I0003474

High Tech

What Actually Happened ?

in Plain English

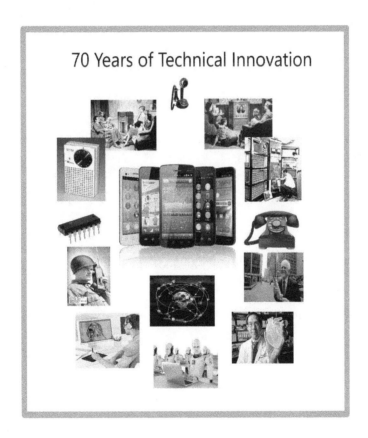

70 Years of Technical Innovation

High Tech

What Actually Happened ?
in plain English

By Ted Di Salvo

Copyright © 2019 Ted Di Salvo

All rights reserved

Except as permitted under the United States Copyright Act of 1976

No part of this publication may be reproduced or distributed in an form or by any means, or stored in any database or retrieval system without explicit prior written permission of the publisher

123456789 HDHD 987654321

Acknowledgments

The author wishes to thank several people for their help in reviewing this book. My family Marian, Christine and Thea for their encouragement. A special thank to my friend and former colleague Bill L'Hotta from the time we worked together at Bell Labs, whose critiques helped immensely in putting this book together.

Table of Contents

Introduction

A very long list of major innovations have occurred during the last 100 years, all leading up to today's technologies. At this point, there doesn't seem to be an end in sight. And there isn't.

The recent major technological advances which appeared in various high tech areas seemed to have occurred in parallel. However, most of these innovations were actually dependent on other seemingly unrelated breakthroughs.

Most "breakthroughs" are usually the result of research and a series of small developments over a long period of time. Sometimes the functionality has been in place for a very long time, just in a different form.

Today's "High Tech Revolution" can be traced to a single major development. The **transistor** in the 1940s.

While this current High Tech revolution is certainly a **game changing** event, there have been others in the past. Looking back at really **High Tech Innovations,** which have had a huge impact and spawned many other remarkable discoveries and industries over the past few hundred years. Each have rippled into multiple innovations and have affected the entire world's societies:

The following excerpts were found in various sites on the internet:

1250-1300: Mechanical Clock:

Hourglass and water clocks had been around for centuries and Sundials in 3500 BC. The first mechanical clocks began to appear in Europe toward the end of the 13th century and were used in cathedrals to mark the time when services would be held.

The following are excerpts from:
https://www.history.com/news/11-innovations-that-changed-history

Printing Press:

*Prior to the rise of the Internet, no innovation did more for the spread and the democratization of knowledge than Johannes Gutenbergs **printing press**. Developed around **1440** in Mainz, Germany, Gutenbergs machine has improved on already existing presses through the use of a mould that allowed for the rapid production of lead alloy type pieces. This assembly line method of copying books enabled a single printing press to create as many as 3,600 pages per day. By **1500** over 1,000 Gutenberg presses were operating in Europe, and by **1600** they had created over 200 million new books.*

Magnetic Compass:

Magnetic compasses *may have been made somewhat obsolete by satellites and global positioning systems, but their impact on early navigation and exploration was inestimable. Originally invented in China, by the **14th** century compasses had widely replaced astronomical means as the primary navigational instrument for mariners. The compass provided explorers with a reliable method for traversing the world's oceans, a breakthrough that ignited the Age of Discovery and won Europe the wealth and power that later fueled the Industrial Revolution. Most importantly, the compass allowed for interaction, both peaceful and otherwise, between previously isolated world cultures.*

Paper Currency:

Throughout much of human history, money took the form of precious metals, coins and even raw materials like livestock or vegetables. The inception of paper money ushered in a bold new era, a world *in which currency could purchase goods and services despite having no intrinsic value. **Paper currency** was widely used in China in the **ninth century**, but did not appear in Europe until the late **1600s**.*

*By the late **19th century,** many nations had begun issuing government-backed legal tender that could no longer be converted into gold or silver. The widespread use of paper currency ushered in a new era of international monetary regulation that changed the face of global economics. Perhaps even more importantly, paper currency was the vital first step in a new monetary system that led to the birth of credit cards and electronic banking.*

Steel:

*While early human societies made extensive use of stone, bronze and iron, it was steel that fueled the Industrial Revolution and built modern cities. Evidence of steel tools dates back 4,000 years, but the alloy was not mass-produced until the invention of the Bessemer Process, a technique for creating steel using molten pig iron, in the **1850s**. Steel then exploded into one of the biggest industries on the planet and was used in the creation of everything from bridges and railroads to skyscrapers and engines. It proved particularly influential in North America, where massive iron ore deposits helped the United States become one of the world's biggest economies.*

Electric Light:

*Pioneered in the early **19th century** by Humphrey Davy and his carbon arc lamp, electric lights developed throughout the **1800s** thanks to the efforts of inventors like Warren de la Rue, Joseph Wilson Swan and Thomas Alva Edison. It was Edison and Swan, who patented the first long-lasting light bulbs in **1879** and **1880**, liberating society from a near-total reliance on daylight. Electric lights went* on to be used in everything from home lighting and street lamps to flashlights and car headlights. The complex networks of wires erected to power early light bulbs also helped lead to the first domestic electrical wiring, paving the way for countless other in-home appliances

Antibiotics:

A giant step forward in the field of medicine, antibiotics saved millions of lives by killing and preventing the growth of harmful bacteria. Scientists like Louis Pasteur and Joseph Lister were the first to recognize and attempt to combat bacteria, but it was Alexander Fleming who made the first leap in antibiotics when he accidentally discovered the bacteria-inhibiting mold known as penicillin in **1928**. Antibiotics proved to be a major improvement on antiseptics, which killed human cells along with bacteria, and their use spread rapidly throughout the **20th century**. Nowhere was their effect more apparent than on the battlefield: While nearly 20 percent of soldiers who contracted bacterial pneumonia died in World War I, with antibiotics, namely Penicillin, that number dropped to only 1 percent during World War II. Antibiotics, including penicillin, vancomycin, cephalosporin and streptomycin have gone on to fight nearly every known form of infection, including influenza, malaria, meningitis, tuberculosis and most sexually transmitted diseases.

The Steam Engine:

Cars, airplanes, factories, trains, spacecraft, none of these transportation methods would have been possible if not for the early breakthrough of the steam engine. The first practical use of external combustion dates back to **1698**, when Thomas Savery developed a steam-powered water pump. Steam engines were then perfected in the late **1700s** by James Watt, and went on to fuel one of the most *momentous technological leaps in human history during the Industrial Revolution. Throughout the **1800s** external combustion allowed for exponential improvement in transportation, agriculture and manufacturing, and also powered the rise of world superpowers like Great Britain and the United States. Most important of all, the steam engines basic principle of energy-into-motion set the stage for later innovations like internal combustion engines and jet turbines, which prompted the rise of cars and aircraft during the 20th century.*

1903 Airplane:

On December 17 Orville Wright made the first airplane flight, of 120 feet, near Kitty Hawk, North Carolina. He and his brother Wilbur made four flights that day. On the last, Wilbur flew 852 feet.

Of course, the development of the Transistor in **1947,** led to further remarkable innovations, such as the integrated circuits and microprocessor, etc.. Other high technology fields, then flourished because of the semiconductor industries. Like home computers, printers, communications and software development. But, that's only part of the impact of today's technological revolution, it's effects spread out to other fields of discovery: all areas of research, teaching, medical advances, space exploration, an uncountable variety of household products,etc. and on to change the social fabric of the entire world.

This book tries to put the events of this current revolution into perspective by providing context and the impact of the various innovations starting around the **1940s.**

Chapter 1: Digital Integrated Circuits

a. The trans-resistor[1]

Make no mistake, the Transistor started this high tech revolution, about 60+ years ago and it continues to today.

Excerpts from: How it works.com/transistors

> *If cells are the building blocks of life, **transistors** are the building blocks of the digital revolution. Without transistors, the technological wonders you use every day -- cell phones, computers, cars -- would be vastly different, if they existed at all.*

Looking back now, the **transistor** seems like a very humble and even an arcane device. The original patent called it : Semiconductor amplifier; three-electrode circuit element utilizing semi conductive materials. The name was later changed to the **transistor.**

The Bell labs team received the 1956 Nobel Prize for Physics.

Figure 1 Inventors of the Transistor at Bell Labs

---

[1] The transistor was at one time early on referred to as the trans-resistor

Excerpts from : CED in the History of Media Technology
The first transistor was invented at Bell Laboratories on
December 16, 1947 by William Shockley (seated at
Brattain's laboratory bench), John Bardeen (left) and
Walter Brattain (right). This was perhaps the most
important electronics event of the 20th century, as it later
made possible the integrated circuit and microprocessor
that are the basis of modern electronics.

While this book deals largely with digital devices and computers, the invention of the transistor also caused similar innovations and advancements in the analog area. Such as radio, TV, stereos, etc..

Numerous variations, improvements and the specialty versions of transistors were eventually developed over time. Just a few of them are:

    Schottky Transistor - Faster speed
    Field Effect Transistor - Closely resembled Vacuum tube
    Darlington Transistor - Higher amplification

Each of the Transistor variations has advantages in certain applications. There is a wealth of information about today's many types of transistor available on the internet. Two such websites are:

    https://www.elprocus.com/different-types-of-transistor-and-their-functions/

    https://www.answers.com/Q/What_are_the_various_ty pes_of_transistors

Figure 2 Current day discreet transistor

The physical size of an individual transistor[2], even today, is immense by integrated circuit standards. Individual transistors are part of a category of electronic parts referred to as discreet components. To illustrate, if you needed 5 transistors to make up a logic gate such as an **AND**[3] or **NAND** gate it would take 5 discrete transistors and a bunch of other components, all individually soldered to a circuit board probably around 2 by 4 inches in size[4].

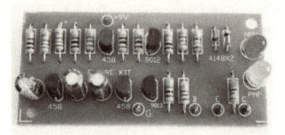

Figure 3 Typical small circuit board utilizing discrete transistors and other components

The advent of the transistor, however was a giant step forward in computer hardware design. The transistor was far superior to the vacuum tube, which had been used in the design of computers up to this point. The newly designed transistor based computer soon became the standard. These computers ran faster, took less space, used less electrical power and were cooler than the vacuum tube based predecessor.

Excerpts from :www.historyofinformation.com

---

[2] The smaller discrete transistors today are little less than a 1/4 inch cube, with three wires protruding in order to be soldered to a circuit board.
[3] A simple logic circuit which has two inputs and one output. When both inputs are a logical high signal, the output is high. This is called an AND gate. When both input signals are high, the output is low. This is called a **NOT AND** or **NAND** gate.
[4] Note: modern surface mount technology would reduce the size of that circuit board by around 50%.

In November 1953 the UK's University of Manchester's experimental Transistor Computer became operational for the first time. This appears to be the first stored-program computer to use mainly transistors as switches rather than vacuum tubes. The transition from vacuum tubes to transistors in computer design was generally delayed because of reliability problems in early transistor manufacturing. ***There were considerable reliability problems with the early batches of transistors and the average error free run in 1955 was only 1 1/2 hours.***

Figure 4 TRADIC Computer - Bell Labs

Excerpts from: https://www.computerhistory.org
J. H. Felker and J. R. Harris work on the Bell Labs TRADIC
computer© *2006-2007 Alcatel-Lucent. All rights reserved*

During the 1950s, semiconductor devices gradually replaced vacuum tubes in digital computers. By 1960 new designs were fully transistorized.
Of course, these computers compared to their predecessors, the vacuum tube computers, transistorized computers were a huge advancement. However, by today's standards, used what amounted to a lot of electrical power. A computer built using discrete transistors with minimal processing power would take up

4

a room. In fact, they did take up a room and the early ones were made by Bell Labs, RCA and the Philco Corporation, to name a few.

For a better view of the "state of the art" computers between the 1950's and the 1990's, the following excerpts found on the web, were from an article entitled "**15 huge supercomputers that were less powerful than your cell phone**"

Excerpts from:
https://www.theclever.com/15-huge-supercomputers-that-were-less-powerful-than-your-smartphone/

➢ *Control Data Corporation (CDC), the company that invented the CDC-1604, sold a whopping 50 of them between 1960 and 1964. They cost around $750,000 apiece, or about $5 million each in today's dollars.*

➢ *Seymour Cray, pretty much ruled the super-computing world. He was the Elon Musk of the "Mad Men" era. While working for the CDC, he designed the first true supercomputer, the CDC 6600. Released in 1964, the 6600 was three times as fast as its closest competitor.*

➢ *The CM-5 supercomputer hit the Top500 list in 1993, with 59.7 gigaflops[5] of processing power—still way short of today's Samsung Galaxy cell phone. Massachusetts-based Thinking Machines Corporation (TMC) was the market leader in parallel supercomputers for a few short years in the late 1980s.*

➢ *While Deep Blue wasn't the fastest supercomputer in the world in 1997—its 11.38 gigaflops of processing speed made it the 259th most powerful—it was probably the most famous. Even though its processing power doesn't*

---

[5] A gigaflop is equal to one billion floating-point operations per second. Floating-point operations are the calculations of floating-point numbers, for example: 2 x 10 to the 3rd power divided by 6 x 10 to 2nd power.

come close to the Galaxy S5 smartphone's 142 gigaflops, Deep Blue utilized its total resources to beat the best chess player in the world, Garry Kasparov, trumping him 2:1 in a six-game chess match.

b. The integrated circuit (IC)

Probably the second biggest breakthrough in the High Tech story was the integrated circuit.
This is where the discrete transistors and other related components were put onto single semiconductor wafer substrate. This was a process which allowed the transistors and some other components to be literally **printed** onto a single silicon wafer.

From: From Wikipedia, the free encyclopedia

*An **integrated circuit** or **monolithic integrated circuit** (also referred to as an **IC**, a **chip**, or a **microchip**) is a set of electronic circuits on one small flat piece (or "chip") of semiconductor material that is normally silicon. The integration of large numbers of tiny transistors into a small chip results in circuits that are orders of magnitude smaller, faster, and less expensive than those constructed of discrete electronic components. The IC's mass production capability, reliability, and building-block approach to circuit design has ensured the rapid adoption of standardized ICs in place of designs using discrete transistors*

Figure 5 Silicon wafer containing hundreds of integrated circuits

Excerpts from:
ethw.org/Milestones:First_Semiconductor_Integrated_Circuit_(IC),_1958

> *On 12 September 1958, Jack S. Kilby demonstrated the first working integrated circuit to managers at Texas Instruments.*
>
> *Today, integrated circuits are the fundamental building blocks of virtually all electronic equipment.*
>
> *The integrated circuit is the invention that enabled the modern electronics industry. Originally used in military applications, it quickly became the core of commercial and consumer electronics. It is estimated that the average person encounters thousands of integrated circuits every day. Because of this invention, the electronics industry has grown from $29 billion in 1961 to $1500 billion today.*

Early Integrated digital logic circuits used what was called resistor-transistor logic gates or RTL. The next generation was called DTL, diode transistor logic and then TTL, transistor transistor logic. Today, TTL is still the logic in use with various speed and other enhancements.

Figure 6 Typical Integrated Circuit

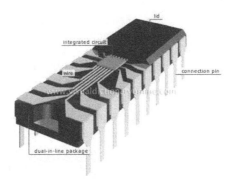

Figure 7 An Illustration of the inside view of a typical Integrated Circuit

As shown in the above figure, the "chip" or silicon wafer with the circuit "printed" or etched onto it is mounted in the integrated circuit "carrier". The carrier has the protruding wires along each side of the carrier, allowing it to be soldered to a circuit board. The integrated circuit is a small monolithic "chip," which may be as small as a few square centimeters or only a few square millimeters. The individual circuit components on the chip are generally microscopic in size.

Over time the integrated circuit improved in speed, capacity and used less power. Some of the variations of digital integrated circuits, which were used in special applications are:

➢   High Threshold Logic (**HTL**), operates at a higher voltage level than TTL and is used in a high electrical noise environment, for example in electrical motor control areas.

➢ Complementary metal–oxide–semiconductor, abbreviated as **CMOS**, is a technology for constructing integrated circuits. CMOS technology is used in microprocessors, micro-controllers, static RAM, and other digital logic circuits.

➢ The integrated Schottky logic (**ISL**) circuit was produced by semiconductor manufacturer Texas Instruments. During 1988, Texas Instruments released a standard transistor-transistor logic (TTL), Schottky, and low power Schottky (LS) devices. The Schottky has a very fast switching action

➢ A field-programmable gate array (also called a field programmable logic array, **FPLA**) is an integrated circuit designed to be configured by a customer or a designer after manufacturing hence "field-programmable". The **FPGA** configuration is generally specified using a hardware description language, similar to that used for an application-specific integrated circuit.

➢ The Metal-Oxide-Field-Effect-Transistor or **MOSFET** was a significant improvement in transistor technology. The Modern monolithic Integrated Circuits are predominantly MOS integrated circuits, built from MOSFETs (metal-oxide-silicon field-effect transistors). The first MOSFET was invented by Mohamed Atalla and Dawon Kahng at Bell Labs in 1959. The earliest experimental MOS Integrated circuit to be fabricated was a 16-transistor chip built by Fred Heiman and Steven Hofstein at RCA in 1962. General Microelectronics later introduced the first commercial MOS integrated circuit in 1964.

c. Computer packaging technology

Advances in packaging may not seem earth shattering, yet they were important and contributed to the overall state-of-the-art. Technical improvements were also occurring in the packaging of electronic components.

Through-Hole Mounting (**THM**) is the process by which component leads are placed into drilled holes on a bare PCB[6]. The process was standard practice until the rise of surface mount technology (SMT) in the 1980s.

The increasing space limitations gave rise to Surface mount technology, and with it, a new era of more compact and

portable electronic devices. The individual electronic components packaging design also changed to what is called Surface Mounted Components.

Figure 8 Through-Hole vs Surface Mount components

Surface mounting technology (**SMT**) was originally called *planar mounting* and was developed in the **1960**s by IBM.

SMT became widely used in the mid **1980**s and by the late **1990**s, the great majority of high-tech electronic printed circuit assemblies were dominated by surface mount devices.

Figure 9 Surface mount components on a circuit board

---

[6] A Printed Circuit Board is a thin board made of fiberglass, composite epoxy, or other laminate material. Conductive pathways are etched or "printed" onto board, connecting different components on the PCB, such as transistors, resistors, etc..

d. Large Scale Integration

The next truly significant innovation came with what is referred to as Large Scale Integration (LSI). Initially, the integrated circuit manufacturing industry suffered from very low yields. That is, a significant number of integrated circuits would fail shortly after manufacturing. It took a number of years before the yields slowly but steadily improved.

Improvements in manufacturing along with smaller sized transistors and the ability to manufacture on larger silicon substrates, along with the ability to produce multiple layer circuits greatly advanced the transistor density and lowered prices.

The following information was found in various places on the internet:

*Moore's law - In **1965**, Gordon Moore, the co-founder of Fairchild Semiconductor and CEO of Intel made a prediction that the number of transistors in a high density integrated circuit would double about every two years. He further said that this rate would continue for the next 10 years.*

Remarkably, the predicted rate of increase pretty much held steady for nearly 35 years, from 1975 until around 2012 (the rate was faster during the first decade).

*Over those 35 years, transistor sizes have decreased dramatically. The number of transistor on a chip has increased a million times. As of 2016, typical silicon chip areas range from a few square millimeters to around 600 square millimeters, with up to 25 million transistors per square millimeter. This high transistor density is referred to a Large Scale Integration (**LSI**).*

Large Scale Integration was also a catalyst for rapid advances in software programming.

Before LSI, software application programs had been somewhat restricted due to the high cost and slow speed of random access memory. When memory storage became less and less expensive and operated at faster and faster speeds, programming in higher level languages began to take off. The higher level languages use a lot more memory, but the programs are much easier to write. This in turn allowed more people to become programmers and generate more complex programs.

e. Custom LSI

LSI was also the catalyst for major advances in audio equipment, appliances, automobile, radio and communications technology. As LSI manufacturing matured, custom LSI chips were offered. A custom LSI chip allowed any company to take their existing electronic circuits and miniaturize it, saving their manufacturing cost and improving reliability of their product in the process.

Customized LSI had a drastic effect on many industries who had any electronics in their products. Companies across the board from the auto industry, appliance manufacturers, every household item imaginable eventually used this technological advancement to improve their products.

Chapter 2: Computers

Contemporary computers, starting about 70 years ago obviously went through many changes. This chapter attempts to not only chronicle it, but explain the events or innovations which caused the changes.

a.   Main Frames

The early computers were what is referred to as **Main Frame computers**.

Excepts from :
https://www.computerhope.com/jargon/m/mainfram.htm
> *Alternatively referred to as a **big iron computer**, a **mainframe** is a large central computer with more memory, storage space, and processing power than a standard computer. A mainframe is used by governments, schools, and corporations for added security and processing large amounts of data, such as consumer statistics, census data, or electronic transactions. Their reliability and high stability allow these machines to run for a very long time, even decades.*

The following web site has what seems to be a rather complete history of computer through the years
https://www.computerhistory.org/timeline/1942/
Some excerpts of early computers are listed below:

➤   1950 - One of the first commercially produced computers, the 1101, designed by ERA, but built by Remington-Rand, was intended for high-speed computing and stored 1 million bits on its magnetic drum, one of the earliest magnetic storage devices.

- 1951 - The Univac-1 is the first commercial computer to attract widespread public attention. Although manufactured by Remington Rand, the machine was often mistakenly referred to as "the IBM Univac." Univac computers were used in many different applications, but utilities, insurance companies and the US military were major customers. Created by Presper Eckert and John Mauchly -- designers of the earlier ENIAC computer -- the Univac-1 used 5,200 vacuum tubes and weighed 29,000 pounds. Remington Rand eventually sold 46 Univac-1s at more than $1 million each.

Figure 10 Univac Computer

- 1952 - The IBM 726 was an early and important practical high-speed magnetic tape system for electronic computers. The Model 726 was initially sold in 1953 with IBM's first electronic digital computer, the Model 701, and could store 2 million digits per tape—an enormous amount at the time. The model 726 rented for $850 a month.

Figure 11 Magnetic Storage Tape

➢ 1953 - MIT's Whirlwind becomes the first computer to use magnetic core memory. Core memory is made up of tiny "donuts" made of magnetic material strung on wires in a grid. Each core stored a bit, magnetized one way for a "zero," and the other way for a "one". In **1971**, the introduction of the Intel 1103 DRAM[7] integrated circuit signaled the beginning of the end for magnetic core memory in computers.

Figure 12 Magnetic Core Memory

b. The Input and Output

Generally, a **mainframe** computer had several users working at computer terminals performing their tasks.

The Teletype machine (**TTY**), which was invented in 1924, and phased out in the 1970s, were used in every major corporation and news room around the world for communications. It was a natural fit as a computer terminal for early computer systems. They provided input and output of data to the computers. Some Teletype machines had built in paper tape punches and readers used to save data or program information from the computer. Also the paper tape punch and reader allowed a previously punched tape of information to be automatically inputted to the computer.

Figure 13 Teletype Machine with a paper tape punch and reader

---

[7] Dynamic Random Access Memory is a type of computer memory which requires less physical space to store the same amount of data as the magnetic core.

15

The Teletype machine went by the wayside after the introduction of the video terminal, it quickly took over the input and output interface of choice for computers. The model VT52 was a CRT-based computer terminal introduced by Digital Equipment Corporation in July 1974. It provided a display with 12 rows and 80 columns of upper-case text, and used an expanded set of control characters and forward-only scrolling based on the earlier VT05.

Figure 14 Digital Equipment's VT52

Usually, a mainframe computer with several users had one and maybe two printers on-line. The user would have to go to the **print room** or where the common printer was located to pick up their printouts rather than have their own printer.

Figure 15 Typical printer using sprocket feed fan-fold paper

As mainframe computers became more advanced, faster and provided more storage, more and more user's video terminals were simultaneously supported. At the same time, the main frame computer was also slowly taking up less and less floor space

Main frame computers required a staff of people behind the scenes to operate of at least one system administrator plus hardware and software maintenance technicians to keep the system operating. Additionally, staff personnel would maintain a **print room** just to distribute the computer printouts requested by the users and keep the printers operational.

At some colleges, students taking computer courses had to submit what was called **batch jobs**[8] as part of their classes. Early on, the batch jobs consisted of a stack of **punch cards**, which described the program they were submitting as part of their homework.

From Wikipedia, the free encyclopedia

*A **punched card** or **punch card** is a piece of stiff paper that can be used to contain digital data represented by the presence or absence of holes in predefined positions. Digital data can be used in data processing applications or, in earlier examples, used to directly control automated machinery.*

From the invention of computer programming languages up to the mid-1970s, most computer programmers created, edited and stored their program line by line on punched cards.

Many early programming languages, including Fortran, Cobol and the various IBM assembler languages, used only the first 72 columns of a card — a tradition that traces back to the IBM 711 card reader used on the IBM 704/709/7090/7094 series.

Punched cards were widely used through much of the 20th century in the data processing industry, where specialized and increasingly complex unit record machines, organized into semiautomatic data processing systems, used punched cards for data input, output, and storage. Many early digital computers used punched cards, often prepared using keypunch machines, as the primary medium for input of both computer programs and data.

The following is from:
https://www.computerhope.com/jargon/p/punccard.htm

---

[8] A **batch file** or **batch job** is a collection, or list, of commands that are processed in sequence often without requiring user input or intervention. Batch job were scheduled to run at certain times, often at off hours.

*Punch cards are known to be used as early as **1725** for controlling textile looms. The cards were later used to store and search for information in 1832 by Semen Korsakov. Later in **1890**, Herman Hollerith developed a method for machines to record and store information on punch cards to be used for the US census. He later formed the company we know as **IBM**.*

While punched cards are now obsolete as a storage medium, although as recently as of 2012, some voting machines still used punched cards to record votes

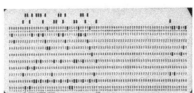

Figure 16 Typical punch card

A punch card machine could punch the holes in the punch cards and have the ability to read the information from the punched card back into the computer. The cards were used

to provide permanent storage of either a computer program or computer information such as input data, customer names and the like.

Figure 17 Typical punch card machine

c. Mini-Computers

From Wikipedia, the free encyclopedia

*A **minicomputer**, or colloquially **mini**, is a class of smaller computers that was developed in the mid-1960s and sold for much less than mainframe and* mid-size computers from IBM and its direct competitors. In a 1970 survey, The New York Times suggested a consensus definition of a minicomputer as a machine costing less than US$25,000 (equivalent to $161,000 in 2018), with an input-output device such as a teleprinter and at least four thousand words of memory, that is capable of running programs in a higher level language, such as Fortran or BASIC.

Minis were designed for control, instrumentation, human interaction, and communication switching as distinct from calculation and record keeping. During the two decade lifetime of the minicomputer class (1965–1985), almost 100 companies formed and only a half dozen remained.

The definition of minicomputer is vague with the consequence that there are a number of candidates for the first minicomputer. An early and highly successful minicomputer was Digital Equipment Corporation's (**DEC**) 12-bit PDP-8, which was built using discrete transistors and cost from US$16,000 upwards when launched in 1964. Later versions of the PDP-8 took advantage of small-scale integrated circuits.

Digital Equipment Corporation (**DEC**) gave rise to a number of minicomputer companies along Massachusetts Route 128, including Data General, Wang Laboratories, Apollo Computer, and Prime Computer.

Figure 18 **DEC**'s PDP-11 Mini-Computer

When single-chip CPU microprocessors appeared, beginning with the Intel 4004 in 1971, the term *"minicomputer" came to mean a machine that lies in the middle range of the computing spectrum, in between the smallest mainframe computers and the microcomputers. The term "minicomputer" is little used today; the contemporary term for this class of system is "midrange computer", such as the higher-end SPARC, Power ISA and Itanium-based systems from Oracle, IBM and Hewlett-Packard.*

Mid-1980s and 1990s saw the decline of the mini-computer.

*The decline of the **mini-computer** happened due to the lower cost of **microprocessor**, the emergence of inexpensive and easily deploy-able local area network systems, and the desire of end-users to be less reliant on inflexible minicomputer manufacturers and IT departments or "data centers". The result was that minicomputers and computer terminals were replaced by networked workstations[9], file servers and PCs in some installations, beginning in the latter half of the 1980s.*

During the 1990s, the change from minicomputers to inexpensive PC networks was cemented by the development of several versions of Unix[10] and Unix-like systems that ran on the Intel x86 microprocessor architecture. Also, the Microsoft Windows series of operating systems included server versions that supported features required for servers.

As microprocessors have become more powerful, the CPUs built up from multiple components – once the distinguishing feature differentiating mainframes and

---

[9] A workstation (WS) is a computer dedicated to a user or group of users engaged in business or professional work. It includes one or more high resolution displays and a faster processor than a personal computer (PC).

[10] UNIX is a popular multi-user, multitasking operating system (OS) developed at Bell Labs in the early 1970s. Due to its portability, flexibility, and power, UNIX has become a leading operating system for workstations.

mid-range systems from microcomputers – have become increasingly obsolete, even in the largest mainframe computers.

Digital Equipment Corporation (DEC) was once the leading minicomputer manufacturer, at one time the second-largest computer company after IBM. But as the minicomputer declined in the face of generic Unix servers and Intel-based PCs, not only DEC, but almost every other minicomputer company, including Data General, Prime, Computervision, Honeywell and Wang Laboratories, many based in New England (hence the end of the Massachusetts Miracle), also collapsed or merged. DEC was sold to Compaq in 1998, while Data General was acquired by EMC Corporation. Compaq later was bought by Hewlett-Packard.

d. The Microprocessor

The advent of the microprocessor is the second Major Advancement of the today's high tech environment.

Excerpts from:
http://www.science.smith.edu/~jcardell/Courses/EGR328/Readings/uProc%20Ovw.pdfA
The microprocessor is one of the most exciting technological innovations in electronics since the appearance of the transistor in 1948. This wonder device has not only set in motion the process of revolutionizing the field of digital electronics, but it is also getting entry into almost every sphere of human life. Applications of microprocessors range from the very sophisticated process controllers and supervisory control equipment to simple game machines and even toys.

The microprocessor or microcomputer is a complete computer processor within a single integrated circuit. It contains the Central Processing Unit (**CPU**), Random Access Memory (**RAM**), Input and Output ports (**IO**), registers, control unit (**CU**) and a data bus.

e. So what is a computer processor ?

The technical description of the basic components of microprocessor architecture includes:

➢ The Arithmetic Logic Unit (**ALU**) performs all arithmetic and logic operations.
➢ Accumulator: Holds the results of operations performed by the ALU.
➢ Program Counter (**PC**) : Holds the memory address of the next instruction to be executed.
➢ Status, data and address registers: The status register stores information about the result of a previous ALU operation, the data register stores data going to or coming from an I/O port or memory, and the address register stores the address of the memory location to be accessed.
➢ Control unit (**CU**): Holds the circuitry that controls the process of executing, decoding and fetching program instructions. Moves data around within the microprocessor.
➢ Data Bus allows the microprocessor to send or receive data to other devices outside of the microprocessor. For example, external memory integrated circuits.

To explain the heart of the microprocessor, also called the central processing unit (**CPU**) even further in plain language this time, consider the following illustration:

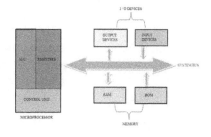

Figure 19 Central Processing Unit Block Diagram

You will be the Central Computer Processor. There are several items available to you:

➤ A list of instructions numbered 1 thru let's say 100. They are the equivalent to the computer instructions, in other words the program to be executed. You have a program counter to keep track of which step, 1 thru 100 you are currently working on.

List of Instructions:

1	Get first number from memory location 17
2	Get second number from memory location 15
3	Add first and second numbers
4	Save the results in memory location 27
5	Get first number from memory location 5
6	Get second number from memory location 26
7	Compare the first a second numbers
8	If the first number is larger than the second number change the program counter to 35

35	More instructions
36	More instructions
Etc.	Etc.
100	End of instructions

Figure 20 List of instructions (computer program)

➤ Next you have three different colored **post-it** pads to write down numbers. These are the equivalent to registers or temporary storage locations for the numbers being processed. The green post-it is for the first number to be processed, the blue is for the second number and the yellow post-it pad is for saving the results.

Green Post-it for first number	Blue Post-it for second number	Yellow Post-it for results

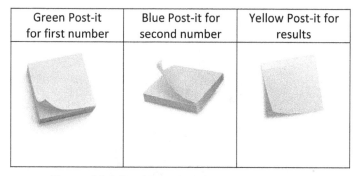

Figure 21 3 Post-it pads (temporary registers)

➢ There is a large bulletin board with numbered squares hanging on the wall next to you. This is the equivalent of the computer's memory.

Figure 22 Bulletin Board (computer memory)

➤ Finally, you have a calculator, which allows you to do the various math or logic operations.

Figure 23 Calculator (Arithmetic Logic Unit)

Now you begin at instruction number one:

Step 1: Get the first number from bulletin board stored in location number 17.

Step 2: Let's say the number you find at location 17 is 255 Write this down on the Green Post-it

Step 3: Get second number from bulletin board stored at Location number 15. Let's say it is 40.

Step 4: Write this number down on the Blue post-it

Step 5: Add the first number and the second number using the calculator. That comes to 295. Write this resulting number on the yellow post-it

Step 6: Save yellow post-it with resulting number on the bulletin board at location 27.

Step 7: Get first number from bulletin board, location number 5. It's the number 7. Write it a green post-it.

Step 8: Get second number from bulletin board location number 26. It is the number 6. Write it on a blue post-it.

Step 9: Compare the first and second numbers.

Step 10: If the first number is larger than the second number change the instruction pointer (program counter) to instruction number 35 and continue executing instructions at that point. If however, the second number is larger, do nothing and go to instruction number 9.

Step 100: End of instructions

The executing of instructions continue until the "end of the program" is encountered, step 100 in above example. Some programs may run in a loop, that is they never actually stop until the power is turned off. For example, the computer may be programmed to continually monitor an alarm button. When alarm button is pressed the computer sends an alert message to the main office. The computer then goes back (loops back to the beginning of the program) and monitors the alarm button.

The central processing unit within a microprocessor or within a mainframe computer operate in the same manner. The program instructions, which get executed, typically contain mathematical instructions such as add, subtract, multiply and divide. Also, instructions can contain logic operations, such as compare the two numbers, greater than, less than, is the number zero, is the number odd or even, etc..

Information is moved from the input or memory locations to temporary registers while the ALU operates on this data. After the ALU performs it's operation, the data is either moved to memory or to the output port.

f. Speech Recognition

Before there was **SIRI**, released by Apple in **2011** and **Alexa** released by Apple in Nov. **2014**, there was a long history of development that came before the Apple Corporation even existed (around **1976**).

The following excerpts were found at:
https://medium.com/swlh/the-past-present-and-future-of-s peech-recognition-technology-cf13c179aaf

➤ In **1879**, **Thomas Edison** invented the first dictation machine, a slightly improved version of his phonograph. In **1886**, **Alexander Graham Bell** created much more user friendly version, using wax cylinders, and promoted the first **dictaphone** to the general public. Dictation machines, capable of recording speech, grew in popularity among doctors and secretaries with a lot of notes to take on a daily basis.

➤ Not until the **1950**s did genuine speech recognition occur. Up to this point, there were attempts at speech creation and recording, but not yet interpretation.

➤ **Audrey**, a machine created by Bell Labs in the **1950**s, could understand the digits 0–9, with a 90% accuracy rate. Interestingly, this accuracy level was only recorded when its inventor spoke; it hovered between 70% and 80% when other people spoke to Audrey.

➤ IBM **Tangora**, released in the mid-**1980**s and named after Albert Tangora, then the world's fastest typist, could adjust to the speaker's voice. It still required slow, clear speech and no background noise, but its use of hidden Markov models allowed for increased flexibility through data clustering and the prediction of upcoming phonemes based on recent patterns. Although it required 20 minutes of training data (in the form of recorded speech) from each user, Tangora could recognize up to 20,000 English words and some full sentences.

➤ **Dragon Dictate**, a consumer product released in **1990** by AT&T. This was deployed for the Voice Recognition Call Processing service in 1992 to route telephone calls without the use of a human operator. The technology was developed by Lawrence Rabiner and others at Bell Labs.

➤ It was only in **1997** that the world's first "continuous speech recognizer" (no longer had to pause between each word) was released, in the form of Dragon's **NaturallySpeaking** software. Capable of understanding 100 words per minute, it is still in use today (albeit in an upgraded form) and is favored by doctors for notation purposes.

➤ By early **2010**s *speech* recognition, also called voice recognition achieved the major breakthrough of speaker independence. Until then, systems required a "training" period.

➤ In **2017**, Microsoft researchers reached a historical human parity milestone of transcribing conversational telephony speech on the widely bench marked Switchboard task. Multiple deep learning models were used to optimize speech recognition accuracy. The speech recognition, word error rate was reported to be as low as 4 professional human transcribers working together on the same benchmark.

Today speech recognition is combined with Artificial Intelligence[11] software to provide a virtual assistant[12]. The well know ones are:

➤ **SIRI** released by Apple in 2011
➤ **Alexa** released by Apple in Nov. 2014
➤ **Cortana** released by Microsoft April 2014
➤ **Google Assistant** released May 2016

---

[11] the capability of a machine to imitate intelligent human behavior
[12] An intelligent virtual assistant or intelligent personal assistant is a software agent that can perform tasks or services for an individual based on commands or questions

g. Fingerprint Recognition

A **fingerprint** is an impression left by the friction ridges of a human finger on surfaces such as glass or metal because of the normally occurring moisture and grease on a finger.

The following excerpts are from:
http://www.ancientpages.com/2016/03/04/fascinating-anc ient-history-of-fingerprints/

> *While it is difficult to establish whether the fingerprints were placed on the artifacts, walls and documents intentionally or coincidentally. The earliest records of fingerprints are seemingly dated to **7000** BC and originate from Jericho, near the Jordan River in the West Bank of the Palestinian.*

> *Fingerprinting seems to have been widely used in the ancient world from China to Persia to Rome to Ireland. According to historians, in **3000** BC the Babylonians would press their fingers into wet clay to record business transactions. The Chinese adapted fingerprint identification by using ink on paper to conduct business transactions and identify their children.*

It wasn't until **1896** when the modern system of fingerprint identification was used by Scotland Yard. In **1903**, the system spread to New York state prisons, further cementing its usage as an investigatory tool.

In **1924** the Federal Bureau of Investigation took over the cataloging of fingerprints in America and by **1971** they had over 200 million fingerprints on file.

In the **1990s** the FBI computerized fingerprinting with the advancements in technology, programs began using Automated Fingerprint Identification Systems. The AFIS's scanned and stored fingerprints electronically.

The following is from Wikipedia the free encyclopedia

> ➢ *In the **1960s**, J. H. Wegstein at the National Bureau of Standards developed computer models for fingerprint*

representations (on cards mainly) to automate their analysis by computer.

➤ *In **1972**, Randall C. Fowler began working in his garage in Redondo Beach, California to develop technology for the acquisition and recording of a persons fingerprints. Several optical techniques were explored and discarded over many months. After a short time Mr. Ken Ruby joined Randy Fowler in his garage and they built prototypes of optical apparatus to acquire and record* 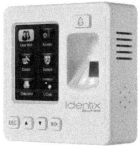 *fingerprints read directly from the finger. The ensuing work produced patented technology, which eventually became the underlying basis for the founding of **Identix** in **1982**.*

Figure 24 Identix Biometric identification Unit

➤ *Founded in **1998** after being spun off from Harris Semiconductor, **AuthenTec** provided mobile security software licenses to mobile manufacturing companies and biometrics sensor technology, such as fingerprint sensors.*

➤ The worlds first fingerprint phone was Pantech Gl100, which launched in **2004**.

➤ In **2007** Toshiba took the fingerprint scanner phones to the mainstream by introducing the Toshiba G500, along with G900.

➤ *In **2012**, Apple acquired AuthenTec, and in Sept. **2013** the iPhone 5S was unveiled, which was the first phone on a major US carrier to feature the technology.*

Fingerprint sensors have changed smart phone security. The ability for the user to unlock their device or get authorization and make payments is something relatively new. Currently there are over 180 devices with fingerprint sensors.

h. Facial Recognition

A facial recognition system is a technology capable of identifying or verifying a person from a digital image or a video frame from a video source. There are multiple methods in which facial recognition systems work, but in general, they work by comparing selected facial features from given image with faces within a database.

During **1964** and **1965**, Woody Bledsoe, Helen Chan and Charles Bisson, worked on using the computer to recognize human faces for an unnamed intelligence agency.

> *"The recognition problem is made difficult by the great variability in head rotation and tilt, lighting intensity and angle, facial expression, aging, etc. Some other attempts at face recognition by machine have allowed for little or no variability in these quantities. Yet the method of correlation (or pattern matching) of unprocessed optical data, which is often used by some researchers, is certain to fail in cases where the variability is great. In particular, the correlation is very low between two pictures of the same person with two different head rotations"* - Woody Bledsoe

By about **1997**, the facial recognition system developed by Christoph von der Malsburg together with graduate students from the University of Bochum in Germany and the University of Southern California outperformed most existing systems at that time. The Bochum system was developed through funding by the United States Army Research Laboratory.

The software was sold as **ZN-Face** and used by customers such as Deutsche Bank and operators of airports and other busy locations. The software was "robust enough to make identifications from less-than-perfect face views. It can also often see through such impediments to identification as mustaches, beards, changed hairstyles and glasses—even sunglasses".

In **2006**, the performance of the latest face recognition algorithms was evaluated in the Face Recognition Grand

Challenge (**FRGC**). High-resolution face images, 3-D face scans, and iris images were used in the tests. The results indicated that the new algorithms are 10 times more accurate than the face recognition algorithms of **2002** and 100 times more accurate than those of **1995**. Some of the algorithms were able to outperform human participants in recognizing faces and could uniquely identify identical twins.

U. S. Government-sponsored evaluations and challenge problems have helped spur over two orders-of-magnitude in face-recognition system performance. Since **1993**, the error rate of automatic face-recognition systems has decreased by a factor of 272. The error rate decreased by one-half every two years.

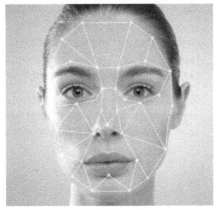

Figure 25 Typical reference points for facial recognition software

In **2009**, the Pinellas County Sherriff's Office created a forensic database that allowed officers to tap into the photo archives of the state's Department of Highway Safety and Motor Vehicles (DHSMV). By **2011**, about 170 deputies had been outfitted with cameras that let them take pictures of suspects that could be cross-checked against the the database. This resulted in more arrests and criminal investigations than would have otherwise been possible.

The world's first face recognition technology for mobile devices with a camera was presented at the Security show Japan in **2005**. The technology named "OKAO Vision Face Recognition Sensor" was created by OMRON corporation.

In **2010**, Facebook began implementing facial recognition functionality that helped identify people whose faces may be featured in the photos that Facebook users update daily.

Apple released the iPhone X in **2017**, advertising face recognition as one of it's primary new features. The face recognition system in the phone is used for device security. The new model of iPhone sold out almost instantly, proving that consumers now accept facial recognition as the new gold standard for security.

Although face unlocking has existed as far back as 2011, with Google's face unlock feature in its Android 4.0 Ice Cream Sandwich OS and Samsung Galaxy Nexus phone, the feature was easy to bypass. Today, Samsung phones like the Galaxy Note 9 offer secure iris scanning alongside Google's face unlock tool and a third method, a combination of the two to unlock phones faster and more accurately.

Apple's method, called **FaceID**, uses an infrared camera, a depth sensor and a dot projector to map out 30,000 points on your face and create an artificial 3D scan.

i. Other Computer Peripherals

Many other computer peripherals have been developed from the 1940s to this day that are worth mentioning. Probably one of the better known is a *pointer* device. There are several varieties all of which perform the same task of directing a pointer on the computer screen to the desired position, which then allows the user to make a selection by *clicking* one of the control buttons.

While the mouse pointing device was available to the public from about **1973**, it's use did not become widespread until the compatible software applications became available on the home computer around **1984**. Following the **mouse** and **trackball**, the **touch pad** and hand held **wand** became available.

- **Pointer devices: Mouse, trackball, touch pad, Joy Stick & Wand**

The **mouse**, sometimes called a *pointer*, is a hand-operated input device used to manipulate objects on a computer screen. Computer mice come in many shapes and sizes but are all designed to fit either the left or right hand, and be used on a flat surface.

Figure 26 Typical computer mouse

Similar to a computer mouse, the **trackball** has a large ball on top of it, so that instead of moving the mouse across a surface, the user keeps the mouse stationary and moves the ball with a finger.

Figure 27 Typical trackball

A **touchpad** or **trackpad** is a pointing device featuring a tactile sensor, a specialized surface that can translate the motion and position of a user's fingers to a relative position on the Computer screen. Touchpads are a common feature of laptop computers as opposed to using a mouse on a desktop, and are also used as a substitute for a mouse where desk space is scarce.

Figure 28 Touch pad built in to Lap Top computer

The electrical two-axis **joystick** was invented by C. B. Mirick at the United States Naval Research Laboratory (NRL) and patented in **1926**. However, not until **the golden age of arcade video games (1978** to **1982)** did joysticks find their

way to the public domain in a major way. Video arcades with large, graphics-decorated coin-operated machines were common at malls and became very popular. Then came affordable home consoles such as the Atari 2600 and Intellivision enabling people to play games on their home TVs during the **1980s.**

Figure 29 Commodore joystick

In **2013**, the eighth generation of game consoles emerged, including Nintendo's **Wii U (hand held Wand)** and Nintendo 3DS, Microsoft's Xbox One, and Sony's PlayStation 4 and PlayStation Vita.

Figure 30 Nyko Wand Controller

The following are excerpts from **Wikipedia, the free encyclopedia - Computer mouse**

➢ The trackball, a related pointing device and forerunner of the mouse, was invented in **1946** by Ralph Benjamin. The device was patented in **1947**, but only a prototype using a metal ball rolling on two rubber-coated wheels was ever built. The device was developed and used for military operations and was kept secret for some time.

Figure 31 Prototype of original mouse

➢ The first public demonstration of a mouse controlling a computer system was in **1968**.

➢ The Xerox Alto was one of the first computers designed for individual use in **1973** and is regarded as the first modern computer to utilize a mouse.

➢ By **1982**, the Xerox 8010 was probably the best-known computer with a mouse. Hawley, who manufactured mice for Xerox, stated that "Practically, I have the market all to myself right now"; a Hawley mouse cost $415 at the time.

➢ In **1982**, Logitech introduced the P4 Mouse at the Comdex trade show in Las Vegas, its first hardware mouse

➢ In **1982** Microsoft made the decision to make the MS-DOS program Microsoft Word mouse-compatible, and developed the first PC-compatible mouse. Microsoft's mouse shipped in **1983**, thus beginning the Microsoft Hardware division of the company.

➢ **The mouse remained relatively obscure until the appearance of the Macintosh 128K (which included an updated version of the Lisa Mouse) in 1984, and of the Amiga 1000 and the Atari ST in 1985.**

Over time, mice grew more ergonomic and have adopted trackballs, lasers pointers, joysticks and hand held wands. Mice and the rest of the *pointers* are connected to a computer either with a cable or wirelessly and are very much in use today.

- **Scanner, FAX machine, Optical Character Reader & handwriting recognition**

The FAX **machine** and **scanner** basically both make copies of documents or pictures without concern to the content of the document. The **Optical Character Reader** and the hand **writing recognition** systems go one step further in that they both are very concerned with the content of the document.

The following excerpts are from Techwalla
https://www.techwalla.com/articles/the-history-of-computer-scanners
And from Wikipedia, the free encyclopedia - **Computer Scanners**

➤ *Scanners owe their existence to the concept of telephotography, a technology based on telegraphs, only instead of simple text, entire images can be transmitted. The principle method involved radio or phone signals using different intensities to depict various tones and colors, gradually forming an image. Telephotography became main stream in the early 20th century, and by the **1920's** Western Union and other service providers had telephotographers in-house at many locations.*

➤ *In **1913** inventor Edouard Belin began working on the technology circa **1905**. Modern scanners entered the market in the **1980's**, although resolutions (measured in dots per inch, or DPI) remained low until the late **1990's**.*

➤ The first image scanner developed for use with a computer was a drum scanner. It was built in **1957** at the US National Bureau of Standards by a team led by Russell A. Kirsch. The first image ever scanned on this machine was a 5 cm square photograph of Kirsch's then-three-month-old son, Walden. The black and white image had a resolution of 176 pixels on a side

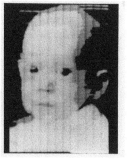

Figure 32 By Russell A. Kirsch - National Institute of Standards and Technology, Public Domain

➤ **1957** - The first modern scanner is the flatbed scanner. It is also widely referred to as a Xerox machine.

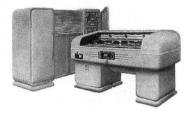

Figure 33 **1957** - Xerox machine.

➤ *Microtek introduced the first model capable of 300 DPI in **1985**, which was a black and white device. Flatbed scanners, with more complex mechanics and capabilities, were later in coming to consumers. Companies such as Acer, Microtek and HP began offering models in the late **1980's**, although hi-res (600 DPI or more), color versions didn't become popular until the mid **1990's**.*

Home-users required scanners until the arrival of digital cameras---people used to scan photos for storage on a PC or for emailing. Digital devices have eliminated the need for this, and cheap all-in-one printers/fax machines mean less demand for document scanning. Currently, scanners remain useful to commercial entities---mainly in publishing.

- **FAX**

The following are excerpts from various articles found on the web regarding the history of FAX technology

> *The first **FAX** device was developed in early **1840s** by the Scottish inventor Alexander Bain. Several years earlier, Samuel Morse had invented the first successful telegraph machine and the fax machine closely evolved from the technology of the telegraph.*

> *In **1860**, a fax machine called the Pantelegraph, invented by Giovanni Caselli, sent the first fax between Paris and Lyon.*

> *In **1914**, Edouard Belin established the concept of the remote fax for photo and news reporting.*

> *In **1924**, the telephotography machine (a type of fax machine) was used to send political convention photos long distance for newspaper publication. It was developed by the American Telephone & Telegraph Company (AT&T) who worked to improve telephone fax technology.*

> *By **1926**, RCA invented the Radiophoto that faxed by using radio broadcasting technology.*

> *On March 4, **1955**, the first radio fax transmission was sent across the continent.*

> *In **1964** Xerox Corporation introduced LDX (Long Distance Xerography), an invention that is considered the first commercial version of today's fax machine.*

> *In **1985** that GammaLink introduced the first computer-based fax board, the GammaFax. The GammaFax was a major advancement, as it brought computers into the worldwide network of fax machines.*

While the FAX technology peaked in use from the late **1980s** to the mid **2000's**, the fax machine is still widely used in a large number of businesses. FAX-ing is now accessible through the internet, via email and web-based interfaces, instead of hardware and phone line based fax machines.

- **Optical Character Reader & handwriting recognition**

The following are excerpts from Wikipedia, the free encyclopedia - **Optical Character Recognition**

Optical character recognition or *optical character reader (OCR) is the electronic or mechanical conversion of images of typed, handwritten or printed text into machine-encoded text, whether from a scanned document, a photo of a document, a scene-photo or from subtitle text superimposed on an image*

Widely used as a form of data entry from printed paper data records, for example: passport documents, invoices, bank statements, computerized receipts, business cards, mail, printouts of static-data, or any suitable documentation. OCR is a common method of digitizing printed texts so that they can be electronically edited, searched, stored more compactly, displayed on-line, and used in machine processes such as cognitive computing, machine translation, (extracted) text-to-speech, key data and text mining. OCR is a field of research in pattern recognition, artificial intelligence and computer vision.

Early optical character recognition may be traced to technologies involving telegraphy and creating reading devices for the blind.

- ➢ *In 1914, Emanuel Goldberg developed a machine that read characters and converted them into standard telegraph code. Concurrently, Edmund Fournier d'Albe developed the Optophone, a handheld scanner that when moved across a printed page, produced tones that corresponded to specific letters or characters.*

- ➢ *In the late 1920s and into the 1930s Emanuel Goldberg developed what he called a "Statistical Machine" for searching microfilm archives using an optical code recognition system. In 1931 he was granted USA Patent for this invention and the patent was later acquired by IBM.*

- ➢ *In 1974, Ray Kurzweil and the company Kurzweil Computer Products, Inc. released the omni-font OCR, which could recognize text printed in virtually any font.*

Kurzweil decided that the best application of this technology would be to create a reading machine for the blind, which would allow blind people to have a computer read text to them out loud. On January 13, 1976, the successful finished product was unveiled during a widely reported news conference headed by Kurzweil and the leaders of the National Federation of the Blind.

➢ *In the 2000s, OCR was made available online as a service (WebOCR), in a cloud computing environment, and in mobile applications like real-time translation of foreign-language signs on a smartphone. With the advent of smart-phones and smartglasses, OCR can be used in internet connected mobile device applications that extract text captured using the device's camera.*

Commissioned by the U.S. Department of Energy (DOE), the Information Science Research Institute (ISRI) had the mission to foster the improvement of automated technologies for understanding machine printed documents, and it conducted the most authoritative of the Annual Test of OCR Accuracy from 1992 to 1996.

Recognition of Latin-script, typewritten text is still not 100% accurate even where clear imaging is available. One study based on recognition of 19th- and early 20th-century newspaper pages concluded that character-by-character OCR accuracy for commercial OCR software varied from 81% to 99%; total accuracy can be achieved by human review or Data Dictionary Authentication.

Recognition of hand printing, cursive handwriting, and printed text in other scripts (especially those East Asian language characters) are still the subject of active research. The MNIST[13] database is commonly used for testing systems' ability to recognize handwritten digits.

---

[13] The **MNIST database** (Modified National Institute of Standards and Technology database) is a large database of handwritten digits that is commonly used for training various image processing systems

j. Storage Devices

Along with the microprocessors, advancements were occurring with computer peripheral: printers, storage devices etc. as well.

I. Internal Storage

A few definitions before discussing computer memory:

Computers use binary[14] numbers internally. That is, *all* calculations, data storage, etc. is in binary code. Ones and zeros.

➢   A **bit** is a single digit, either 1 or 0

➢   A **byte** of binary information consist of 8 bits (**10101010**). This byte represents anywhere from **0** to **255** in decimal.

➢   A *word* is generally referring to 2 bytes of binary information or 16 bits (**1010101010101010**), which is the equivalent of **0** to **65535** in decimal. The computer term **word** can also be used to describe the width of the data bus or internal CPU registers, such as a 32 or 64 bit **word** computer processor or data bus.

➢   **Hexadecimal** numbers, which is a well used coding convention, uses 4 bits of binary information (**1010**) representing **0, 1,2,3,4,5,6,7,8,9, A, B, C, D, E, F**. Keep in mind this is only a coding convention, the computer itself still only used ones and zero.

➢   A one thousand byte memory is designated as 1KB and it means 1000 memory locations, each location having a single byte or 8 bits of information. Therefore, for example 64KB is 64,000 memory locations, each with 8 bits of information. A 1MB is one million memory locations, each having 8 bits of data.

---

[14] There were some attempts to use different coding, but binary is by far the most prevalent.

> The following table illustrates numbers 0 to 15 in binary, hexadecimal and decimal.

Binary	Hexadecimal	Decimal
0000	0	0
0001	1	1
0010	2	2
0011	3	3
0100	4	4
0101	5	5
0110	6	6
0111	7	7
1000	8	8
1001	9	9
1010	A	10
1011	B	11
1100	C	12
1101	D	13
1110	E	14
1111	F	15

Figure 34 Binary vs Hexadecimal vs Decimal

Just for information (**there will NOT be a quiz later**). A byte in hexadecimal representation would require 2 hexadecimal digits. For example the binary number **10101011** would be **AB**, which is equal to **171** in decimal. Much more information on this subject can be found on the internet. A table is shown, in figure 24, to illustrate numbers 0 to 15 in binary, hexadecimal and decimal.

II. Random Access Memory

Excerpts from "Timeline of Computer Memory"
  Bellis, Mary. "History of Computer Memory."
   Thought Co, Feb. 23, 2019,
   thoughtco.com/history-of-computer-memory-1992372.
   https://www.thoughtco.com/history-of-computer-memor
   y-1992372

➢   **1942** - *The Atanasoff-Berry Computer has 60 50-bit words of memory in the form of capacitors mounted on two revolving drums. For secondary memory, it uses punch cards.*

➢   **1947** - *Frederick Viehe of Los Angeles applies for a patent for an invention that uses magnetic core memory. Magnetic drum memory is independently invented by several people:*
   • *An Wang invented the magnetic pulse controlling device, the principle upon which magnetic core memory is based.*
   • *Kenneth Olsen invented vital computer components, best known for "Magnetic Core Memory" Patent No. 3,161,861 and as being the co-founder of Digital Equipment Corporation.*
   • *Jay Forrester was a pioneer in early digital computer development and invented random-access, coincident-current magnetic storage.*

➢   **1949** - *Jay Forrester conceives the idea of magnetic core memory as it is to become commonly used, with a grid of wires used to address the cores. **The first practical form manifests in 1952-53 and renders obsolete previous types of computer memory.***

➢   **1966** - *Hewlett-Packard releases their HP2116A real-time computer with 8K of memory. The newly formed Intel starts to sell a semiconductor chip with 2,000 bits of memory.*

➢   **1968** - *United States Patent and Trademark Office grants patent 3,387,286 to IBM's Robert Dennard for a* *one-transistor DRAM cell. DRAM stands for Dynamic RAM (Random Access Memory) or Dynamic Random Access Memory. DRAM will become the standard memory chip for personal computers replacing magnetic core memory.*

➢ *1969 - Intel begins as chip designers and produces a 1 KB RAM chip, the largest memory chip to date. Intel soon switches to being notable designers of computer microprocessors.*

➢ *1970 - Intel releases the 1103 chip, the first generally available DRAM memory chip.*

➢ *1971 - Intel releases the 1101 chip, a 256-bit programmable memory, and the 1701 chip, a 256-byte erasable read-only memory (EROM).*

➢ *1974 - Intel receives a U.S. patent for a "memory system for a multichip digital computer".*

➢ *1975 - Personal consumer computer, Altair was released. It uses Intel's 8-bit 8080 processor and includes 1 KB of memory. Later in the same year, Bob Marsh manufacturers the first Processor Technology's 4 kB memory boards for the Altair.*

➢ *1984 - Apple Computers releases the Macintosh personal computer. It is the first computer that came with 128KB of memory. The 1 MB memory chip is developed.*

Semiconductor Random Access Memory (**RAM**) means the information within the memory's locations may be read or written to in any order. That is the memory does not need to be accessed in sequence.

Another version of semiconductor RAM, called DRAM[15] which can achieve very high densities, thus making DRAM much cheaper per bit. Today billions of memory locations can fit on a single memory chip. The downside of DRAM is it consumes relatively large amounts of power.

---

[15] Dynamic Random Access Memory

Semiconductor memory started out as what's referred to as volatile memory, meaning the information saved in the memory would be lost if the electrical power was removed. This was not the case with it's predecessor, magnetic core memory which would not lose information if the power were removed. There were, however, significant drawbacks with magnetic core memory: they were very slow, consumed a lot of power and offered poor storage density.

Despite magnetic core memory's shortcomings, it was used extensively until around 1987 because it was non-volatile. For a short while there were some memory circuit boards which had a built in battery so the volatile memory would hold it's data.

Both the *battery backup* and the *core memory* technology were eventually replaced by EEPROM, the semiconductor version of non-volatile memory. An electrically erasable, programmable, read-only memory **EEPROM** uses voltage to erase memory.

➢ Toshiba developed **flash memory** from EEPROM (electrically erasable programmable read-only memory) in the early 1980s, and then commercially introduced it to the market in **1987**.

➢ **Non-volatile random-access memory (NVRAM)** is random-access memory that is non-volatile. Development is going on for the use of NVRAM chips as a system's main memory, for a more persistent memory. Known as NVDIMM-P, released in **2018**.

For further information, see:
Non-volatile random-access memory - From Wikipedia, the free encyclopedia

The following excerpts found on:
https://computer.howstuffworks.com/computer-memory2. htm

> *Today's computers use combinations of different types of memory within the same computer. Some of the types of RAM in use today is:*

> *Dynamic RAM **(DRAM)** requires a periodic 'refresh' of power in order to not loose it's stored data. DRAM's advantages are lower costs of manufacturing and greater memory capacities.*

> *Static RAM **(SRAM)** doesn't need to be 'refreshed' to remember the data being stored. The advantages of using SRAM are lower power consumption and faster access speeds.*

> *Flash Memory is a type of non-volatile storage medium that retains all data after power has been cut off.*

> ***Graphics Double Data Rate Synchronous Dynamic RAM (GDDR SDRAM).*** *Released in **2003** is specifically designed for video, graphics rendering, typically in conjunction with a dedicated GPU (graphics processing unit) on a video card.*

III. Read Only Memory

Read Only Memory (**ROM**) is computer memory which cannot be changed or written-to. Read only memory is permanent memory just like a punched card or a punched tape. The ROM does not forget it's information when the power is turned off and back on.

Read Only Memory is obviously used for programs or fixed data which will not change during the program's execution. Fixed computer memory is used in many control devices, like a microwave oven or a dishwasher. Where the program function is always the same, like a rinse cycle.

That's not to say the computer in such devices has only permanent memory. It usually has both changeable memory, RAM and permanent memory ROM. The RAM would be used for a user entered parameter, like how long to run the microwave and the power level setting: low, medium or high. The computer would then use the fixed memory (the program) for the procedural part of the cycle and use the variable time period selected by the user. A calculator would be a perfect example of the need for dual types of memories.

The following is excerpts are from:
https://www.computerhistory.org/siliconengine/semiconductor-read-only-memory-chips-appear/

> *In **1965** Sylvania produced a 256-bit bipolar TTL ROM for Honeywell that was programmed one bit at a time by a skilled technician at the factory who physically scratched metal link connections to selected diodes. Production orders were satisfied with custom-mask programmed devices. Also in 1965 General Microelectronics developed slower, but four-times larger 1024-bit ROMs using MOS technology.*

> *By the early 1970s Fairchild, Intel, Motorola, Signetics, and TI offered 1024-bit TTL ROMs, while AMD, AMI, Electronic Arrays, General Instrument, National, Rockwell and others produced 4096-bit (4K) MOS devices.*

> *Desktop calculators were the first high-volume application, which was then surpassed by video game cartridges that used hundreds of millions of 16K and larger devices from U. S. and Japanese vendors. Production of Nintendo's first Super Mario Brothers NES game alone exceeded 40M units. As each ROM is manufactured to order, customers were often frustrated with long delivery times and vendors overwhelmed by production logistics. Relief came in the form of user-programmable ROMs (PROMs).*

> A **programmable read-only memory (PROM)** is a form of digital memory where the setting of each bit is locked by a fuse or anti-fuse[16]. It is one type of ROM (read-only memory). The data is "burnt-in" and cannot be changed. The user programmable read only memory (**PROM**) was invented in 1956 by Wen Tsing Chow, working the American Bosch Arma Corporation. Although

---

[16] An Anti-fuse is an electrical device that performs the opposite of a fuse. An Anti-fuse permanently creates an electrical connection path.

ant-ifuse-based **PROM** has been available for decades, it wasn't available in standard CMOS until **2001** when technologies using a standard CMOS process, enabling integration of PROM into logic CMOS chips. OTP (one time programmable) memory is a special type of non-volatile memory (NVM) that permits data to be written to memory only once.

➢ **EPROM (Erasable Programmable Read Only Memory)** was a great invention that allowed hardware programmers to make changes to their code without buying new chips. This invention is attributed to Dov Frohman of Intel in **1971.** It was followed by the **Ultraviolet Programmable Read Only Memory (UVPROM)** which is an integrated-circuit memory chip in which the stored information can be erased only by a strong ultraviolet light and the circuit can then be reprogrammed with new information that can be stored indefinitely. This was followed by the **EEPROM** or **Electrically Erasable Programmable Read Only Memory.** The only difference between the two is that you can

 erase an EEPROM with electricity. Although it might seem to be a very small difference, it resulted in major changes that turned the EEPROM into the new standard.

Figure 35 An Ultraviolet ROM has a window for the UV light to erase the memory stored in the chip

Read more about the Difference Between EEPROM and EPROM
http://www.differencebetween.net/technology/difference-between-eeprom-and-eprom/#ixzz5xcXMoY9P

IV. Hard Drives

In **1953**, the engineers at IBM's San Jose, California laboratory invented the hard disk drive. The disk drive created a new level in the computer data hierarchy, then termed "Random Access Storage", but today known as secondary storage. It was less expensive and slower than main memory (then typically magnetic drums) but faster and more expensive than tape drives.

It had **5** megabits of storage, weighed over 2000 pounds and leased for $3500/month in 1957. One thousand units were produced until 1961 and the product was withdrawn in 1967.

Figure 36 IBM RAMAC - Hard Disk Storage 1957

Introduced in **1970**, the **DIRECT ACCESS MAGNETIC DISC STORAGE DEVICE**, invented by Goddard & Lynott from the IBM RAMAC program is generally considered to be the fundamental patent for disk drives.

The following is from "The History of Hard Disk Drives"- *Wikipedia, the free encyclopedia*

➢ *In **1964**, Burroughs introduced the B-475 disk drive*

➢ *In **1970**, IBM introduced the 2305 disk drive*

➢ *In **1973**, IBM introduced the IBM 3340 "Winchester" disk drive, the first significant commercial use of low mass and low load heads with lubricated platters and the last IBM disk drive with removable media.*

➢ Also in **1973**, *Control Data Corporation introduced the first of its series of Storage Module Drive (SMD) using conventional disk pack technology. The SMD family became the predominant disk drive in the minicomputer market into the* **1980**s.

➢ *The IBM PC XT in* **1983**, *included an internal standard 10MB hard disk drive, and soon thereafter internal hard disk drives proliferated on personal computers.*

Figure 37 Hard Disk Drive - cover removed to show disk

➢ *In* **2001** *the Hard Disk Drive industry experienced its first ever decline in units and revenue. The number of manufacturers decreased to 6 in 2009 and 3 in 2013. Unit production peaked in 2010 at about 650 million units and has been in a slow decline since then. Shipments in 2017 were estimated at about 404 million units.*

Solid State Drives (SSD) began appearing In **1995**. M-Systems introduced flash-based solid-state drives as Hard Disk Drive replacements for the military and aerospace industries.

In **2018**, both Samsung and Toshiba introduced to market 30.72 Terabytes Solid State Drives . Nimbus Data announced and reportedly shipped 100 Terabyte drives using a SATA[17] interface. Hard Disk Drives are not expected to reach that capacity until 2025.

Figure 38 Solid State Drive

---

[17]   SATA is a Serial computer bus technology for connecting hard disks and other devices.

In 1991 the storage capacity of Hard Disk Drives was around 20 megabytes and in 2018 around 100 terabytes. That is a remarkable 5 million to one improvement is storage capacity, along with a 134,000 to 1 reduction in cost on a per byte basis.

V. Removable Storage

The following are Excerpts from:
Removable media - *From Wikipedia, the free encyclopedia*

> **Removable media** *are a form of computer storage that is designed to be inserted and removed from a system. The earliest form of removable media, punched cards and tapes, predates the electronic computer by centuries, with the Jacquard loom of 1801 using interlinked cards to control the machine. This followed a loom made by Basile Bouchon in 1725 that used paper tape for its instructions. Punched tape was later used in Colossus, the first electronic computer.*

> *Magnetic tape was developed in the early 20th Century in Germany, based on magnetic wire recording invented by Valdemar Poulsen in 1898. In **1951**, the UNIVAC-1 was released, using magnetic tape to store data. 8-inch floppy disks were commercially introduced in **1971** by IBM, with them being compacted to 5 ¼-inch by Shugart Associates in 1976. At the same time Compact Cassettes started being used to store data, being popular in the late 1970s and 1980s for holding data for personal computers. In **1982**, the 3 ½-inch floppy disk became commonplace, with its introduction of the Apple Macintosh and Amiga.*

Figure 39   8 inch, 5 ¼ inch and 3 ½ inch Floppy
Disks and their respective drives

*The CD-ROM was introduced in **1985**, providing much
higher capacity than a floppy disk, however could not be
written to. This was resolved in **1990** with the
introduction of the CD-R. The CD-RW, introduced in **1997**
allowed the CD to be written to multiple times, rather
than just once, as with the CD-R. DVD versions of these*

*formats introduced in the
late 1990s provided further
increases in capacity.
Additional capacity
improvements were
achieved with Blu-ray in
2006.*

Figure 40 CDROM disk being placed in drive

*The turn of the millennium saw the widespread
introduction of solid-state removable media, with the SD
card being introduced in **1999**, followed by the USB flash
drive in **2000**. The capacity of these removable flash
drives improved over time, with **2013** seeing Kingston
unveiling a 1 terabyte USB flash drive.*

VI. How is information stored in a drive?

Taking the cover off a hard disk drive reveals the following critical components: The **magnetic platters (disks)**, stacked on top of each other. The magnetic **read/write heads** between each of the magnetic disk platters. Note the heads do not actually touch the surface of the magnetic platters, but are extremely close. The **armature** move the heads in and out of the magnetic disk platters.

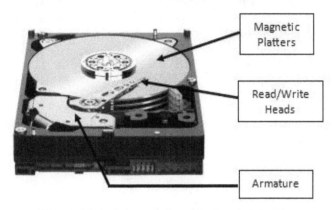

Figure 41 An internal view of a hard disk drive

The information being read and written to the magnetic disk platters is the index and the data or files to be stored.

The variations of File Allocation Tables and disk formats are almost endless. For more information about this subject, refer to: **File Allocation Tables - Wikipedia the free online Encyclopedia.**

The following attempts to explain the common basic theory of operation underlying the various FAT and storage schemes.

The storage of information uses the same basic scheme, whether for a hard disk drive, a floppy disk and even a solid state drive. The scheme uses what is called a **File allocation Table (FAT)**.

The following are Excerpts from:
File Allocation Table - From Wikipedia, the free encyclopedia

Each system uses an index table, the File Allocation Table (FAT), which is statically allocated at the time of formatting. The table contains entries for each cluster, a contiguous area of disk storage. Each entry contains either the number of the next cluster in the file, or else a marker indicating end of file, unused disk space, or special reserved areas of the disk. The root directory of the disk contains the number of the first cluster of each file in that directory; the operating system can then traverse the FAT, looking up the cluster number of each successive part of the disk file as a cluster chain until the end of the file is reached. In much the same way, sub-directories are implemented as special files containing the directory entries of their respective files.

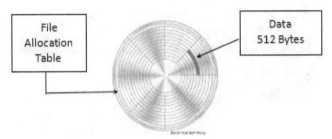

Figure 42 Magnetic Disk with 8 sectors

The physical locations on the disk, which are pie shaped, are sectors 1 through 8. The tracks go completely around the disk from the outermost edge toward the center of the disk and are numbered 1 through 80 or so, depending on the size of the disk.

Simply put, there is an **index (file allocation table)**, which is always in the same location on each type of storage device so the disk reader knows where to find it. The information in the index has the name of the file and the location[18] where it is stored. The data is stored in fixed size data blocks[19]. This location in the index is only the starting location of the data. The location of the next portion of the data is at the end of

---

[18] Track and Sector
[19] Data block sizes are 512 Bytes minimum

the first block of data. Each block of data has a pointer to the location of the rest of the data until the last block of data, which has an end of data marker. Therefore one file, depending on it's size can take many locations on the disk. Further, when a file is deleted, the locations are reused. This often means pieces of a single file can be in many locations anywhere on the disk.

File Allocation Table

Name of File	Track 5 Sector 3

Track 5 Sector 3

Data - first 512 Bytes	Track 5 Sector 4

Track 5 Sector 4

Data - second 512 Bytes	Track 7 Sector 2

Track 5 Sector 3

Data - third 512 Bytes	End of Data

Note: When a file is deleted from the disk storage, only the name of the file and it's starting location in the **index** (**FAT**) are deleted and all the tracks and sectors of that deleted file become available. The consequence of that is **the actual data has not been deleted**. The only way the data would really be gone is if a new file of data overwrites it. This is why some deleted information can be recovered from drives.

k. Printers

The teletype machine which was invented in **1924**, and phased out in the **1970s**, could be considered the first printer and keyboard as it was used by early mainframe computers.

The following excerpts are from:
https://www.computerhope.com/history/printer.htm

> ➢ *In **1953** the first high speed printer was developed by Remington-Rand for use with the UNIVAC computer.*

> ➢ *The first dot matrix impact printer was produced by Centronics in **1970***

> ➢ *The development of the first laser printer was completed in **1971** by Xerox*

> ➢ *Thermal printer, which were for the consumer market became available around **1972** and are still in use for some retail applications, for example at the gas pump or restaurants, etc..*

> ➢ *Hewlett Packard introduced the inkjet printer in **1976**, however it did not gain popularity until the mid-**1980**s.*

> ➢ *The first high speed laser printer was from IBM in **1976**.*

> ➢ *The HP DeskJet inkjet printer was introduced by Hewlett-Packard in **1988** and sold for $1000. It is considered the first mass-marketed inkjet printer and became a very popular and widely used series of printers.*

Many modern 3D printers use a technology called **FDM (fused deposition modeling)**, which was developed and patented by Scott Crump in **1988**. Stratasys, Inc. made available their first 3D printer in **1992**, which is based on FDM (fused deposition modeling) technology, developed and patented by company co-founder S. Scott Crump. The patent on FDM (fused deposition modeling) expired in **2009**, opening the door for an open-source development community, called RepRap, along with other commercial companies, use FDM to develop new 3D.

Three Dimensional Printing is a very significant technical development with potentially a very far reaching impact on our lives. New uses of 3D technology are appearing literally every day.

Figure 43 3 Dimensional printer making specialized parts

The **3D applications are as varied as literally building human organs, building specialized components for prosthetics, building one of a kind parts for various research projects and even building homes.**

Figure 44 3 Dimensional printed human heart

For more information, simply search the internet for "advances in 3d printing in medical field" or just "advances in 3D printing"

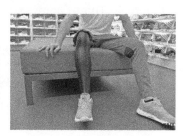

Figure 45 3 Dimensional printed prosthetic

The following are excerpts found on the internet:
https://www.realtor.com/news/trends/3-d-printed-homes/

How 3-D Printers Will Lower Prices, Make Fantasies Real, and Transform the Housing Market

By Clare Trapasso | Aug 31, 2016

Three-dimensional printers will be able to erect homes in days instead of months—making them substantially cheaper to build.

Three-dimensional printing will eventually help facilitate the creation of radical new housing designs, new shapes, and brand-new architectural ideas. The road from fanciful concept to livable reality will become shorter and more traverseable than ever.

Figure 46 Three Dimensional printing a full size house

And we're not talking about a far-distant future. Rudimentary printed structures, mostly made of concrete and resembling stark gray boxes, are already sprouting up around the globe.

And while such current buildings may not exactly be the "dream home" of your average buyer, experts predict that within five to 25 years (depending on whom you're talking to), the technology will be advanced enough to print sophisticated and easily customizable dwellings out of wood, metal, and stone.

Now a handful of cutting-edge construction companies are engaged in something like a 3-D printing arms race—each striving to be the first to refine the technology.

A Chinese company even recently printed a two-story, 4,305-square-foot building on-site in just 45 days.

Figure 47 Complete 3 Dimensional printed home

This printed home's construction cost is about four thousand dollars. The actual printing process took around 24 hours. Put simply, the 3D printer, which looks like a small crane, extrudes cement out of a nozzle in layer after layer to create a structure.

The machine didn't do all the work, though. The roof, insulation, windows, and other components were all added later by conventional construction methods. The total cost for the project came in at just about $10,000, not including furniture or appliances.

l. Desk Top Personal Computer

The microprocessor had a huge impact on the personal computer industry. There was a lot of activity in the desktop computer area early on as is chronicled below:

The following are excerpts from:
https://lowendmac.com/2014/personal-computer-history-the-first-25-years/

➤ *The first personal computers, introduced in **1975**, came as kits: The MITS Altair 8800, followed by the IMSAI 8080, an Altair clone.*

➤ *In **1976**, Apple's two Steves (Jobs and Wozniak) designed the Apple I, Apple's only "kit" computer (you had to add a keyboard, power supply, and enclosure to the assembled motherboard), around the 6502 processor.*

➤ *In **1977** Apple introduced the Apple II, a color computer with expansion slots and floppy drive support; Radio Shack rolled out the TRS-80 to its stores across the nation; Commodore tapped into the pet rock craze with its PET; and the first ComputerLand franchise store (then Computer Shack) opened.*

➤ **1980** was the year Commodore opened the floodgates of home computing with the **$299 VIC-20**. Sinclair tried to one-up them with a **$199** kit computer, the ZX80, which was quite popular in Britain, but it was destined to remain a bit player in the PC industry.

Figure 48 Commodore PET

Estimates are that there were one million personal computers in the US in 1980.

➤ In early 1981, Adam Osborne introduced the first portable computer. The Osborne 1 was about this size of a suitcase, ran CP/M[20], included a pair of 5.25″ floppies, and had a tiny 5″ display. The innovative machine was bundled with about $1,500-2,000 worth of software, and the whole package sold for $1,795 (equivalent to $4,947 in 2018).

Figure 49 The Osborne 1 portable computer

➤ The first laptop computer also arrived in 1981, the Epson HX-20 (a.k.a. Geneva). The HX-20 was about 8.5″ by 11″ and maybe 1.5-2″ thick and used a micro-cassette to store data. It displayed 4 lines of 20 characters on an LCD screen above the keyboard.

Figure 50 Epson HX-20 personal computer

---

[20] CP/M is an operating system widely used on microcomputers to enable a wide range of software from many suppliers to be run on them.

➤ Of course, **the most significant event of 1981 for the personal computing industry was the introduction of the IBM PC on August 12**. This computer ran a 16-bit CPU on an 8-bit bus (the Intel 8088), had five expansion slots, included at least 16 KB of RAM, and had two full-height 5.25" drive bays.

Buyers could get a fairly loaded machine with a floppy controller, two floppy drives, a monochrome display adapter and 720 x 350 pixel green screen monitors, a color

Figure 51 IBM PC

display adapter (CGA) (320 x 200 with 4 colors or 640 x 200 with 2 colors) monitor, a parallel card, a dot matrix printer, and an operating system – with the choice of CP/M-86, the UCSD p-System[21], or PC-DOS[22] (a.k.a. MS-DOS). Pretty much everything was an option, and everyone recognized that the IBM PC was based on ideas perfected in the Apple II, particularly general use expansion slots.

The **second most significant event for the computer industry of 1981 was: Microsoft was able to get IBM agree that PC-DOS would not be an IBM exclusive.** This paved the way for the clone industry, which in the end marginalized the influence of Big Blue.

---

[21] UCSD p-System (**U**niversity of **C**alifornia at **S**an **D**iego p-System) An early software development system designed for cross-platform portability. Source programs (BASIC, Pascal, etc.) were compiled into intermediate "p-code" programs, which were executed by an interpreter in the target machine.
[22] Short for Personal Computer Disk operating system, PC-DOS is a text-based operating system first released by IBM in August 1981.

More information about the history of the personal computer can be found on the following website:
https://lowendmac.com/2014/personal-computer-history -the-first-25-years/

Time magazine called 1982 "The Year of the Computer" as the industry grew up. By 1983, the industry estimated that 10 million PCs were in use in the United States alone.

According to a report by Forrester Research, there were over one billion PCs in use worldwide by the end of 2008, and over 2 billion by the year 2015. These numbers are staggering.

Computers continued to improve in speed, storage, capabilities and all the while the price went down from the mid 1980s to the current day. Of course we now have I-pads, tablets and phones , all with greater capacity than the mainframe computers in the 1980s.

The widespread use of personal computers was a monumental event in high technology. This put computers in the hands of two billion and counting, people around the world. That in turn has lead to countless other developments, research, products, services and applications. Further, the proliferation of inexpensive computers and the free flow of information contributed, perhaps in just a small way, to freedom and prosperity of people around the world.

Huge developments occurred across the board in numerous fields during this time, such as research, internet, space exploration, e-commerce, video disks, automotive, military and software. Some of these breakthrough events were:

➤ The **human genome project** started in **1990** and ended in **2003**. This was 13 years of hard work for the scientists.

➤ Although originally proposed in **1989, the web** was first launched and used in the early **1990s**. Tim Berners-Lee , with help from Robert Cailliau, was able to connect hypertext with the internet and create the foundation for what we know as the web today.

➢ One of the largest telescopes in the world, **the Hubble Space Telescope**, was launched into orbit in **1990**. The Hubble was designed to be maintained and serviced by astronauts and is still operating today.

➢ While the concept of e-commerce existed loosely for a few years, it wasn't until the **1990**s that **modern e-commerce** was born. In **1995**, both **Amazon** and **eBay** launched, and in **1999 Alibaba**[23] made its debut. These sites redefined the shopping experience.

➢ The **digital video disc** (DVD) appeared in the mid to late **1990**s. The superior picture and sound of the DVD helped it quickly disrupt the existing VHS tape market.

➢ The **Prius** was the first **mass-produced hybrid automobile** and it helped popularize hybrid technology and make it accessible to consumers.

➢ The General Atomics MQ-1 Predator has been in use by the US Air Force since **1995**. It piqued much of the public interest and concern over a **drone** and **UAV technology**.

➢ Both TiVO and ReplayTB made their debut at the CES in **1999** and the **digital video recorder** (DVR) was born. The concept quickly gained popularity and is now integrated with the TV itself or available through cable providers.

➢ In the late **1990s**, the first truly portable **MP3 players** were released. The Saehan Information Systems MPMan launched in **1997** and the Diamond Rio PMP300 followed in **1998**.

➢ The **Large Hadron Collider** (**LHC**) is the world's largest and most powerful particle Collider and the largest machine in the world. It was built by the European Organization for Nuclear Research (CERN) between **1998** and **2008** in collaboration with over 10,000 scientists and hundreds of universities and laboratories, as well as more than 100 countries.

---

[23] The Chinese version of Google

Chapter 3: Programming

The following is from Wikipedia, the free encyclopedia:

History of software
https://en.wikipedia.org/wiki/History_of_software

Software is programmed instructions stored in the memory of digital computers for execution by the processor. Software is a recent development in human history, and it is fundamental to the Information Age.

*Charles Babbage's programs for his Analytical Engine in the **19th** century is often considered the founder of the discipline, though both mathematicians' efforts remained theoretical only, as the technology of Babbage's day proved insufficient to build his computer. Alan Turing is credited with being the first person to come up with a theory for software in **1935**, which led to the two academic fields of computer science and software engineering.*

*The first generation of software for early stored-program digital computers in the late **1940s** had its instructions written directly in binary code, generally written for mainframe computers. Later, the development of modern programming languages alongside the advancement of the home computer would greatly widen the scope and breadth of available software, beginning with assembly language, and continuing on through functional programming and object-oriented programming paradigms.*

*The very first time a stored-program computer held a piece of software in electronic memory and executed it successfully, was **11 am on 21 June 1948**, at the University of Manchester, on the Manchester Baby computer.*

It was written by Tom Kilburn, and calculated the highest factor of the integer 2^18 = 262,144. Starting with a large trial divisor, it performed division of 262,144 by repeated subtraction, then checked if the remainder was zero. If not, it decremented the trial divisor by one and repeated the process.

Computers only interpret (understand) ones and zeros, therefore the actual program which a computer directly understands is binary. To write a program in binary is an extremely difficult task, therefore a **mnemonic**[24] language, which is called **assembler**[25] was used.

This mnemonic language consisted of computer instructions which directly referenced the internal registers and arithmetic logic unit of the particular computer being programmed.

Sample commands written in Assembly language would be:
    MOV R1, 34h
Means move the hexadecimal value of 34 into register R1.
Or
    INC AX
Means increment by 1 (add 1) to the contents of the AX register.
Or
    ADD WORD1,3
Means add 3 to the value of stored in memory location WORD1.

Some Arithmetic Instructions would be:
    ADD means add two numbers
    SUB means subtract one number from the other
    INC means increment (add 1) to a number
    DEC means decrement (subtract 1) from a number

Some other commands:
    MOV means move a number from one place to another
    XCHG means exchange two numbers with each other

---

[24] A mnemonic is a term, symbol or name used to define or specify a computing function.
[25] Assembler language is any low-level programming language in which there is a very strong correspondence between the instructions in the language and the particular computer's architecture.

Writing a computer program in assembly language required an extensive knowledge of the internal hardware design of the particular computer processor being programmed. Also, an extensive knowledge of the mnemonic assembler language being used. Finally, programming assembly language required a lot of time and patience, which in *Engineering* is referred to as ***Infinite Attention to Detail***.

Because of this painstaking process and typically a limited amount of (then expensive) computer memory, programs written with assembly language early on were generally not very large or overly complex.

Some excerpts about Assembly Language from:
From Wikipedia, the free encyclopedia

> *Kathleen Booth is credited with inventing assembly language based on theoretical work she began in **1947**, while working at Birkbeck, University of London following consultation by and her then-future husband (Andrew Booth) with John von Neumann and Herman Goldstine at the Institute for Advanced Study.*

> *In late **1948**, the Electronic Delay Storage Automatic Calculator (**EDSAC**) had an assembler (named "initial orders") integrated into its bootstrap[26] program. It used one-letter mnemonics developed by David Wheeler, who is credited by the IEEE Computer Society as the creator of the first "assembler." Reports on the **EDSAC** introduced the term "assembly" for the process of combining fields into an instruction word. **SOAP** (Symbolic Optimal Assembly Program) was an assembly language for the IBM 650 computer written by Stan Poley in **1955**.*

> *Assembly language has long been the primary development language for many popular home computers of the **1980s** and **1990s** (such as the MSX, Sinclair ZX Spectrum, Commodore 64, Commodore Amiga, and Atari ST). This was in large part because*

---

[26] A bootstrap is the program that initializes the computer's operating system during start-up.

interpreted BASIC[27] dialects on these systems offered insufficient execution speed, as well as insufficient facilities to take full advantage of the available hardware on these systems.

In the mid **1960s**, the **BASIC** Computer language made it's appearance. BASIC is a higher level programming language, thus it is easier to understand and use. To illustrate the ease of programming in BASIC the following is the popular simple program written in BASIC:

```
PRINT "Hello, World!"
END
```

This program displays the words "Hello World!" on the computer's video screen.

To write this same program in assembly language would require more steps as the following example shows:

```
DATA SEGMENT
    MESSAGE DB "HELLO WORLD!$"
ENDS
CODE SEGMENT
    ASSUME DS:DATA CS:CODE
START:
    MOV AX,DATA
    MOV DS,AX
    LEA DX,MESSAGE
    MOV AH,9
    INT 21H
    MOV AH,4CH
    INT 21H
    ENDS
END START
```

Some excerpts about BASIC computer Language from:
From Wikipedia, the free encyclopedia
BASIC (Beginner's All-purpose Symbolic Instruction Code) *is a family of general-purpose, high-level programming*

---

[27] Beginners All-purpose Symbolic Instruction Code. A high-level symbolic computer programming language which is commonly used to write programs for PC-type computers.

*languages whose design philosophy emphasizes ease of use. In **1964**, John G. Kemeny and Thomas E. Kurtz designed the original BASIC language at Dartmouth College. They wanted to enable students in fields other than science and mathematics to use computers. At the time, nearly all use of computers required writing custom software, which was something only scientists and mathematicians tended to learn.*

*BASIC fell from use during the late **1980s** as newer machines with far greater capabilities came to market and other programming languages (such as **Pascal** and **C**) became tenable. In **1991**, Microsoft released **Visual Basic**, combining a greatly updated version of BASIC with a visual form builder. This reignited use of the language and "**VB**" remains a major programming language in the form of **VB.NET**.*

Some of the more popular computer languages which came after the assembly language are:

➢ **COBOL** is a programming language that reads like regular English and is often used for business and administrative purposes. The name means Common Business Oriented Language and has been around since the **1950's**, though by the changing standards of technology, it was considered to be old news by the **1980's**. Still, the programming language continues to be used today and shows no signs of fading away anytime soon.

➢ **FORTRAN** (or formula translation) was the first high-level programming language (software) invented by John Backus for IBM in **1954**, released commercially in **1957**. FORTRAN is still used today for programming scientific and mathematical applications.

➢ **Pascal** (named in honor of the French mathematician, philosopher and physicist Blaise Pascal) became very successful in the **1970s**, notably on the burgeoning minicomputer market.

➢ The **C** programming language displaced the **Pascal** language during the late **1980s** and early 1990s as UNIX-based systems became popular.

➢ The first version of **Small-Talk** software to be made publicly available and created in **1980**. Small-Talk is an object-oriented[28] programming language that use "classes" is sometimes called class-based programming.

➢ In **1985**, the first commercial edition of *The C++ Programming Language* (an Object Oriented Language) was released, which soon became the definitive reference for the language.

➢ **LISP** is a family of computer programming languages with a long history and a distinctive, fully parenthesized prefix notation. Originally specified in **1958**, **LISP,** which stands for **LIST-Processor,** is the second-oldest high-level programming language in widespread use today. It quickly became the favored programming language for artificial intelligence (AI) research. As one of the earliest programming languages, **LISP** pioneered many ideas in computer science, including tree data structures, automatic storage management, dynamic typing, conditionals, higher-order functions, recursion, the self-hosting compiler, and the read–eval–print loop.

Aside from computer programming languages, another area of software which had a significant effect on software development was the computer's operating system[29]. Operating systems simplify human interaction with the computer hardware. They are responsible for linking

---

[28] **Object-oriented programming (OOP)** is a programming paradigm based on the concept of "objects", which can contain data, in the form of fields (known as *attributes or properties),* and code, in the form of procedures (known as *methods).*

[29] An **operating system** (OS) is **system** software that manages computer hardware, software resources, and provides common services for computer programs. Time-sharing **operating system' s** schedule tasks for efficient use of the **system** and may also include accounting software for cost allocation of processor time, mass storage, printing, and other resources.

71

application programs with the hardware, thus achieving easy user access to computers. Two operating systems, in particular had the greatest impact on future software development progress.

The first was **UNIX**, which was mainly used in mainframe computers. The second popular operating system was **DOS**, which was used on personal desktop computers. These two operating system became very popular and allowed the development of many new software applications.

The following excerpts were from the "History of UNIX"
From Wikipedia, the free encyclopedia

> **UNIX** developed at Bell Labs by Ritchie and Thompson and was first presented formally to the outside world at the **1973** Symposium on Operating Systems Principles. **UNIX** was one of the first operating systems to be written in a high-level programming language, namely C. This meant that it could be installed on virtually any computer for which a C compiler existed. This natural portability combined with its low price, made it a popular choice among universities. It was inexpensive because antitrust regulations prohibited Bell Labs from marketing it as a full-scale product.

The following excerpts were from the "MS-DOS"
From Wikipedia, the free encyclopedia

> **MS-DOS (Microsoft Disk Operating System)** was a renamed form of 86-DOS – owned by Seattle Computer Products, written by Tim Paterson. Development of 86-DOS took only six weeks, as it was basically a clone of Digital Research's CP/M (for 8080/Z80 processors), ported to run on 8086 processors. This first version was shipped in August 1980 Microsoft, which needed an operating system for the IBM Personal Computer hired Tim Paterson in May **1981** and bought 86-DOS 1.10 for $75,000 in July of the same year. Microsoft kept the version number, but renamed it MS-DOS. They also licensed MS-DOS 1.10/1.14 to IBM, who, in August 1981, offered it as PC DOS 1.0 as one of three operating systems for the IBM 5150, or the IBM PC.

These two operating systems, **UNIX** and **MS-DOS** became hugely popular and were widely used. This was a significant point in software applications development and resulted in a number of what were called "**killer Applications**".

In **1972**, *Pong - Video Games Arrive.* Atari introduced the first commercially successful video game – Pong. Based on ping pong (table tennis), Pong was a simple game which hooked up directly to a television set.

Speaking of *killer apps,* the following excerpts taken from:
Top 10 Most Important Software Programs by John C. Dvorak 2004:

> ➤ *Software took center stage in **1978** when Dan Bricklin and Bob Frankston produced VisiCalc, the first electronic spreadsheet. This turned the personal computer into a useful business tool, not just a game machine or replacement for the electric typewriter. **VisiCalc** and its descendants, including Lotus 1-2-3 and Microsoft Excel, were standout products. While fundamentally not as important as word processing, the modern spreadsheet, initially implemented on the Apple II, became the triggering mechanism that brought what was then called a microcomputer into the office. **Almost all of the history of desktop computing stems from this invention.***

> ➤ ***dBASE II (1980)--A remarkable product in its day, and its influence lives on in all low-end commercial database software.*** *It popularized the concept of a relational database manager, although it didn't quite follow all the parameters.*

> ➤ ***WordStar (1978-1979)**—WordStar and its predecessor the **Electric Pencil**, as well as descendants, such as **Microsoft Word** for Windows, have to be included. **WordPerfect** also deserves a mention here. But it was*

WordStar *that really triggered things and became the first word processing, called a "killer app", dominating word processing for over a decade beginning with its release in the late 1970s.*

➤ *Aldus* ***Pagemaker*** *(1985)--This is the program that sealed the deal for desktop publishing and the concept of* ***WYSIWYG***[30]. ***It's the granddad of much of today's layout and design software.*** *Other names in drawing software should be mentioned are* ***Illustrator*** *and* ***Freehand***.

➤ ***Photoshop (1990)***--*Over time the importance of this program to the development of small computers will increase. Used by professionals and amateurs alike,* ***this software has influenced all its competition*** *and has become very desirable.*

➤ ***The Mosaic browser (1993)--This is the code that triggered the second desktop revolution,*** *in combination with the World Wide Web. All modern browsers are based on many of the principles developed by Mosaic.*

Multi-user Operating Systems: This type of Computer operating systems allows multiple users to access a computer system simultaneously. These operating systems were mostly used in **mainframe** situations. **Unix, Solaris, Linux** and **Open VMS** are examples of multi-user operating systems.

Single-user operating systems, as opposed to a multi-user operating system, are usable by only one user at a time. Single user operating systems would be found mostly in **desktop** or **lap top** computers. **Mac OS (released in 1978)** and **Windows (released in 1985)** are examples of single-user operating systems.

Mobile Operating System: Although not functionally distinct from desktop operating systems, the **mobile OS** is definitely

---

[30] What You See Is What You Get

an important type of operating system. A mobile operating system supports wireless communications and mobile applications. It has built-in support for mobile multimedia formats. Tablets and Smart Phones run on mobile operating systems. **Apple's iPhone operating system (released in 2007)** and **Google's Android (released in 2011)** are well known names of mobile operating systems.

Chapter 4: Communications

a. The Telephone

The 1940s was a big year for advancement in communications. The first **public telephone** came out in the 1940s. Also the **television, telegraph**, and **teletype** became available in retail for people to buy and use. The television quickly became the most popular item in this decade.

Some of the following excerpts regarding the telephone were taken from the internet including:

https://bebusinessed.com/history/history-of-the-telephone

> *The rotary dial phone[31] was actually introduced with the first commercial installation of a 99-line automatic telephone exchange in La Porte, Indiana, in 1892.*

Figure 52 Replica of a Candle Stick Rotary Dial Phone

> *In 1878 the First Telephone Book was released soon after the world's first telephone line was invented. That first telephone book, released by the New Haven District Telephone Company, was just one page long and held 50 names. The book did not list any numbers. If you needed to call someone, you just said that person's name and the operator would connect you.*

---

[31] The user put a finger in the holes in the dial and moves the rotary dial to the end position and then releases the dial.

> The desk top rotary dial phone appeared around the **1930s**. Phone manufacturers started combining the mouthpiece and receive into a single unit.

Figure 53 Typical Desk Top Rotary Dail Phone

> The rotary dial was gradually supplanted by push button phone[32] after it's introduced to the public at the **1962** World's Fair under the trade name "Touch-Tone". Touch-tone technology primarily

used a keypad in the form of a rectangular array of push-buttons for dialing.

Figure 54 Typical Push Button Desk Phone

The following excerpts were taken from:
http://www.telephonetribute.com/timeline.html

> **1949** - AT&T introduces the famous black rotary Model 500 telephone.

> **1949** - Dialing of **transcontinental telephone calls** by operators started with the joining of toll dialing networks on East and West coasts.

> **1949** - The volume of telephone calls reaches **180 million a day!**

> **1950 - 75% of telephone are party lines[33].**

> **1956** - The Bell System and the British Post Office inaugurates service on a **transatlantic telephone cable** called **TAT-1**.

---

[32] The first touch tone phone was actually invented in **1941**, but not available to the public until **1962**.

[33] Party line is up to 4 phones in 4 different homes sharing the same phone line. So only one phone could use the line at a time. The other phones could and sometimes did listen in.

➤ **1970** - Corning Glass demonstrates highly transparent fibers, and Bell Laboratories demonstrate semiconductor lasers that could operate at room temperature; these demonstrations help establish the feasibility of fiber-optic communication. As far back as Roman times, glass has been drawn into fibers. Yet, it was not until the 1790s that the French Chappe brothers invented the first "optical telegraph." It was a system comprised of a series of lights mounted on towers where operators would relay a message from one tower to the next.

b. Computers start talking over the phone lines

Computer communications over the phone lines was another significant advancement. The ramifications of this advancement were far reaching, for an example, the local computer bulletin boards, which later brought the internet.

c. How is information transferred

The communications between the operator of a teletype machine and the computer utilizes what is called **ASCII** code. The acronym **ASCII** stands for American Standard Code for Information Interchange. It is a 7 bit code[34] representing the alphabetic characters, lower and upper case A thru Z, numbers, other symbols such as ! @ # $ %, etc. and a number of unprintable characters.

The speed of the communications between the computer and the teletype is referred to as the **Baud Rate**.

The term **Baud** originates from the French engineer Emile Baudot, who invented the 5-bit teletype code. The **Baud Rate** refers to the number of *signal* or *symbol* changes that occur per second, which is 2 bits.

---

[34] An 8 bit ASCII is also used, called extended ASCII code. Some of these 256 characters are not printable.

Digital communications, in general, follows a simple idea, which can be illustrated using buckets on a conveyor belt as follows:

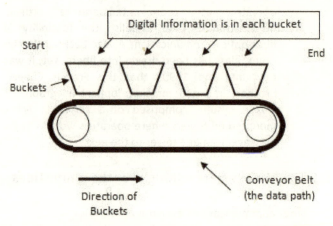

Figure 55 Digital Information travelling in Buckets

The buckets or containers are actually a **digital frame** travelling along the data path. The data path is illustrated as a conveyor belt from the **start** to **end** points. The **frame** for the ASCII teletype communications is defined by a "start bit(s)[35]" and an "end bit(s)".

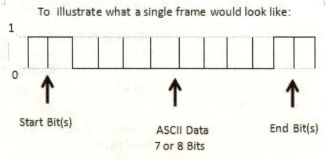

Figure 56 Single ASCII data frame

The ASCII character represented in binary code would be inserted into the frame at the start point of the transmission,

---

[35] Variations use 1 or 2 start bits and 1 or 2 stop bits.

the teletype machine's output, and removed at the end point of the transmission, the computer's input.

In **1963**. Robert Weitbrecht developed a **coupling** device that converted sound from the earpiece of the telephone handset to electrical signals, and converts the electrical pulses coming from the teletypewriter to sound that goes into the mouth piece of the telephone handset.

In telecommunications, an **acoustic coupler** is an interface device for coupling electrical signals by acoustical means, usually in and out of a telephone.

The practical upper limit for acoustically coupled modems was 1200-baud[36], first made available in **1973** by Vadic and **1977** by AT&T. The use of Acoustic couplers became widespread by **1985**.

Figure 57 Teletype with built in acoustic coupler.

Teletype units with acoustic couplers allowed users to remotely access computers. This device enabled the "*work from home*" employee. Also, such devices facilitated the creation of dial-up bulletin board systems, a forerunner of modern internet chat rooms, message boards, and e-mail.

---

[36] Baud is a measure the speed of signaling or data transfer, equal to the number of pulses or bits per second.

The acoustic coupler was eventually replaced by a **modem**[37]
which plugged directly
into the phone line via a
phone jack. The direct
connect modem was
easier to use and more
reliable than an audio
connection through the
phone lines.

Figure 58 The Hayes Modem

The Hayes Smartmodem was released in **1981**. Hayes was a major brand in the modem market with the introduction of the original 300 bit/s. They remained the premier modem vendor throughout the **1980s**, periodically introducing newer, faster modems. Competition, however eventually caught up with Hayes during the **1990s** and Hayes closed it's doors in **1999**.

In telecommunications, **RS-232, Recommended Standard 232** refers to a standard, originally introduced in **1960** for serial communication transmission of data. This standard formally defines signals connecting between data terminal equipment (**DTE**) such as a computer terminal and data communication equipment (**DCE**), such as a modem.

The **RS-232** cable/connector became a standard feature of many types of computers. Personal computers used them for connections not only to modems, but also to printers, computer mice, data storage, uninterruptible power supplies, and other peripheral devices. The **RS-232** is the forerunner of the **USB** connector.

---

[37] Short for modulato-demodulator a **modem** is an electronic device that makes possible the transmission of data to or from a computer via telephone or other communication lines.

d. Introduction of industry standards

Published in **1984** the **ISO[38] 7-layer** communications standard separated a computer's application and communications network system into layers. Each layer had a distinct functionality. Each entity interacted directly only with the layer immediately beneath it, and provided facilities for use by the layer above it.

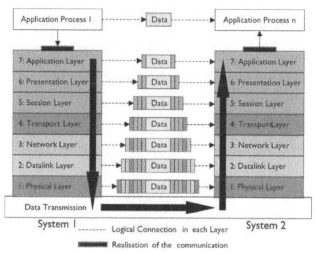

Figure 59 7 Layer communications standard

When two computing systems were communicating back and forth, the individual layers would **only** communicate with it's corresponding layer in the other system. For example, the physical layer, which is the actual hardware connection between the systems, would only be concerned with moving the information across the physical connection and passing or receiving the data from the layer above it. The following diagram describes the functionality of each level in the 7 layer protocol definition.

---

[38] The **Open Systems Interconnection** model is a conceptual model that characterizes and standardizes the communication functions of a telecommunication or computing system without regard to its underlying internal structure and technology.

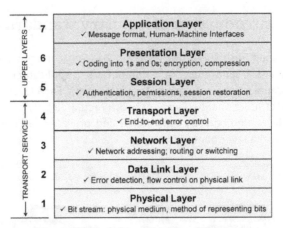

Figure 60 Details of 7 Layer Protocols

The OSI 7 Layer Protocol could be thought of as 7 Buckets or data frames, each getting bigger and bigger as the layers are added. Something like the following generic illustration:

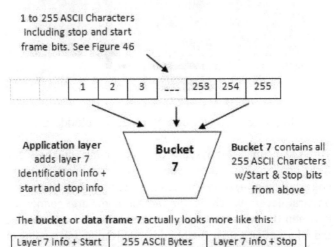

Figure 61 Bucket or Data Frame 7

The **Presentation Layer**, OSI layer 6 takes the **bucket 7** from the layer above and puts it in a slightly bigger **bucket 6**. **Bucket 6** or frame layer number 6 looks something like:

Layer 6 info + Start	Bucket 7	Layer 6 info + Stop

The **Session layer**, OSI layer 5 takes bucket 6 and puts it in a slightly bigger **bucket 5** or frame layer 5.

Bucket 5 or frame layer number 5 looks something like:

Layer 5 info + Start	Bucket 6	Layer 5 info + Stop

This building of frames continues until the lowest layer number 1, the **Physical layer**. The final data frame contains information from each frame and looks something like this:

L1	L2	L3	L4	L5	L6	L7	L6	L5	L4	L3	L2	L1

Again the information contained in frames L1 through L6 only contain layer control and identification info. Frame L7 is the only portion containing actual data **from** or **to** the user.

The OSI 7 Layer reference model was a major advance in promoting the idea of a consistent model of protocol layers.

Without getting mired in the details of each layer, the upper 3 layers dealt with the user of the software application. For example, the user working with a word processor or a spreadsheet on a computer terminal.

The lower 4 layers deals with details of getting the information from the user software application to the remote computer. This remote computing device may be connected via a hard wire, a network (such as the internet) or a wireless connection. The point is transporting the information back and forth is independent of the application the user is working with. Conversely, how the information gets to the remote device is of no consequence to the user of the application.

The transport service layers 1 - 4 provide seamless and error free transmission of the data required for the top level application to perform smoothly. The computer could be connected to another computing device via a phone, a network or the internet.

Further, the transport services also validate the information using a checksum[39] or some other verification method. If an error is detected the transport layer detecting the problem will automatically request a re-transmission of that data frame. This re-transmission is usually why the user may see an occasional delay in the data appearing on the screen.

Unlike the original communications of just ASCII characters going back and forth between a teletype machine and a computer. The data being transferred came to include graphics data as well. There are numerous software **data compression algorithms** to compress this graphical data and allow for faster graphic data transfers.

The significance of this ISO 7 layer protocol allowed for future advancements in communications such as local and wide area networks and of course the internet. Further, this protocol allowed software applications to be developed independently of the transport services software.

ISDN

Another standard, defined in **1988** called **Integrated Services Digital Network (ISDN)** is a set of communication standards for simultaneous digital transmission of voice, video, data, and other network services over the traditional circuits of the public switched telephone network.

ISDN is employed as the network, data-link and physical layers in the context of the **OSI** model. In a video-conference, ISDN provides simultaneous digitized voice, video, and text transmission between individual desktop videoconferencing systems and group (room) videoconferencing systems.

---

[39] A numerical value calculated from a series of bits of digital data, often by summing their values, used to test whether the data has changed during storage or transmission.

The **OSI and ISDN standards,** when used in conjunction with computer networks, enabled multiple users on different computers, in different locations (possibly anywhere in the world), to all work on the same project at the same time. Examples of this could be:

➤ A power point sales presentation given to clients across the country.

➤ Multiple users reviewing the Company's financial results for the past year at each Corporate office in the country.

➤ Comments on a cooperative research report by the document's contributors from the four corners of the globe.

➤ Video conference calls

➤ A game of chess by two masters each at home.

➤ A game of 3D golf with four golfing friends, each on their personal computers in their own home.

e. Networks

A **local area network (LAN)**
is a computer network that
interconnects computers
within a limited area such
as a residence, school,
laboratory, university
campus or office building.

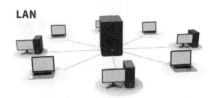

LAN

Figure 62 Local Area Network

In order to have multiple local computers, printers, user
terminals all communicate with each other, a device called a
Router[40] must be added to the system.

Cisco Systems, founded in **1984** released the ASM/2-32EM
router deployed at CERN in **1987.**

This hardware device called a **Router** adds more information
to the previously described **ISO 7 Layer Protocol**. The local
network router by necessity, adds a device identification
number to the data frames, so the information in the frame

ends up at the intended
destination. Therefore, each
device connected to the
Local Area Network must
have an identification or a
unique address, including
the **Router** itself.

Figure 63 Modern hard wired Cisco Router

Over time, hard wired communications speeds increased. The
first **LANs** were connected with coaxial cable, the same type

---

[40] A router is connected to two or more data lines from different
networks. When a data packet comes in on one of the lines, the
router reads the network address information in the packet header
to determine the ultimate destination. Then, using information in its
routing table or routing policy, it directs the packet to the next
network on its journey.

used to deliver cable television. These facilities are relatively inexpensive and simple to attach. More importantly, they provide great bandwidth (the system's rate of data transfer), enabling transmission speeds initially up to 20 megabits per second. Today's speeds, however are in excess of 1000 megabits per second even up to one gigabit per second.

A **Wide Area Network (WAN)** is a telecommunications network that extends over a large geographical area for the primary purpose of computer networking. Wide area networks are often established with leased telecommunication circuits.

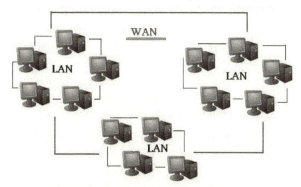

Figure 64 A Wide Area Network connecting to LANs

When one **Local Area Network** is connected to one or more **Local Area Networks** a **Gateway Router** is used for each LAN. Of course, this Gateway Router adds still more "routing" information to the packets of information so the information may be delivered to and from the correct devices in the overall system. As as example, the User working at Computer 35 in LAN-1 is communicating with another user working on Computer 3 in LAN-3, the data packets must go back and forth between those two locations only.

Some common network types:

 ➢ **PAN - Personal Area Network** is a network wherein restrictions are established to promote a secured environment. This type of network can be configured in such a way that devices outside the network cannot access it.

➢ **LAN** - **Local Area Network** consists of a network of personal computers in a small area (such as an office) for sharing resources (such as a printer) or exchanging data

➢ **MAN** - **Metropolitan Area Network** is similar to a local area network (**LAN**) but spans an entire city or campus. **MANs** are formed by connecting multiple **LANs**. Thus, **MANs** are larger than **LANs,** but smaller than wide area networks (**WAN**). **MANs** are extremely efficient and provide fast communication via high-speed carriers, such as fiber optic cables.

➢ **WAN** - **Wide Area Network is** a network of computers (such as the Internet) in a large area (such as a country or the globe) for sharing resources or exchanging data. Wide area networks are often established with leased telecommunication circuits.

➢ **VPN** - **Virtual Private Network** is a private network that is built over a public infrastructure. Security mechanisms, such as encryption, allow VPN users to securely access a network from different locations via a public telecommunications network, most frequently the Internet. In some cases, virtual area network (**VAN**) is a **VPN** synonym.

➢ **Broadband** technically refers to any type of signal transmission technique, either wired or wireless, that carries two or more different types of data in separate channels. For example, a home cable TV service, which provides internet service combining high-speed data with video signals supplied over cable TV lines. In popular usage, however, it refers to any high-speed internet connection.

➢ **Bandwidth** is the capacity for data transfer of an electronic communications system, *especially* : the maximum data transfer rate of such a system

Credit for the initial concept that developed into the World Wide Web is typically given to Leonard Kleinrock. In **1961**, he wrote about ARPANET, the predecessor of the Internet, in a paper entitled "Information Flow in Large Communication Nets."

The following is from Wikipedia, the free encyclopedia:

> The **Advanced Research Projects Agency Network (ARPANET)** was the first wide-area packet-switching network with distributed control. This became the technical foundation of the Internet. The ARPANET was established by the Advanced Research Projects Agency (ARPA) of the United States Department of Defense.
>
> While the **ARPANET** project was initiated in **1966,** the first computers were connected in 1969, and the Network Control Program was implemented in 1970. Networking research in the early 1970s by Bob Kahn and Vint Cerf led to the formulation of the Transmission Control Program (**TCP**) in 1974
>
> Access to the ARPANET was expanded in 1981, when the National Science Foundation (NSF) funded the Computer Science Network (CSNET). In the early 1980s, the NSF funded the establishment of national supercomputing centers at several universities, and provided network access and network interconnectivity with the NSFNET project in 1986. The ARPANET project was formally decommissioned in 1990, after partnerships with the telecommunication industry paved the way for future commercialization of a new world-wide network, known as the Internet.
>
> The ARPANET was operated by the military during the two decades of its existence, until 1990.

All these developments in network communications enabled the success of the World Wide Web.

English scientist Tim Berners-Lee invented the **World Wide Web in 1989**. He wrote the first web browser in **1990** while employed at CERN near Geneva, Switzerland. The browser was released outside CERN in **1991**.

The World Wide Web has been central to the development of the Information Age and is the primary tool billions of people use to interact on the Internet.

The first-ever website (info.cern.ch) was published on **August 6, 1991** by British physicist Tim Berners-Lee while at CERN, in Switzerland. On **April 30, 1993** CERN made World Wide Web technology available on a royalty-free basis to the public domain, allowing the Web to flourish.

In **1994**, there were less than 3,000 websites online. By 2014, there were more than 1 billion. That represents a *33 million percent* increase in 20 years. There are over **1.5 billion websites** on the world wide web today. Of these, it is estimated that 200 million are actually active.

Of course, many of today's corporate giants owe their very existence to the World Wide Web: Google, Amazon, U-Tube and Face Book just to name a few.

Some common World Wide Web terms:

➢ A **Browser** is a free software package or mobile app that displays web pages, graphics, and most online content. Popular web browsers include Chrome, Firefox, Internet Explorer, Microsoft Edge, and Safari, but there are many others.

➢ A **Web Page** is what you see in your browser when you are on the internet. Think of the web page as a page in a magazine. You may see text, photos, images, diagrams, links, advertisements, and more on any page you view.

➢ **Uniform Resource Locators — URLs —** are the web browser addresses of internet pages and files. With a URL, you can locate and bookmark specific pages and files in your web browser.

➢ **HTTP** is the acronym for **Hypertext Transfer Protocol**, the data communication standard of web pages. When a web page has this prefix, the links, text, and pictures should work correctly in your web browser.

➢ **HTTPS** is the acronym for **Hypertext Transfer Protocol Secure.** This indicates that the web page has a special layer of encryption added to hide your personal information and passwords from others.

*Whenever you log in to your online bank account or a shopping site that you enter credit card information into, look for **https** in the URL for security.*

➤ **Hypertext Markup Language (HTML)** is the programming language of web pages. HTML commands your web browser to display text and graphics in a specific fashion.

➤ You need an **Internet Service Provider (ISP)** to get to the internet. You may access a free ISP at school, a library or work, or you may pay for a private ISP at home.

➤ A **Router** or **Router-Modem** combination is the hardware device that regulates the network signals arriving at your home or business from your **ISP**. A **Router** can be wired or wireless or both. **Cable Modems**[41] remains one of the most popular types of high-speed internet access in the U.S., Canada, and other countries. Rated connection speeds of cable internet connections typically range between 20 Mbps[42] and 100 Mbps

➤ **Email** is **electronic mail**. It is the sending and receiving of typewritten messages from one screen to another. Email is usually handled by a web-mail service - Gmail or Yahoo Mail, for example - or an installed software package such as Microsoft Outlook, AOL or Apple Mail.

➤ **Spam** is the jargon name of **unwanted and unsolicited email**. Spam email comes in two main categories: high-volume advertising, which is annoying, and hackers attempting to lure you into divulging your passwords, which is dangerous. Filtering is the popular-but-imperfect defense against spam.

---

[41] Modems may be considered a gateway node in that they are separate WANs from LANS
[42] Million bits per second

*To protect yourself against hackers who want your personal information, be suspicious. Your bank won't email you and ask for your password. That fellow in Nigeria doesn't really need your bank account number. Amazon isn't handing you a free $50 gift certificate. **Anything that sounds too good to be true probably isn't true. If you are unsure, do not click any links in the email and contact the sender (your bank or whomever) separately for validation.***

➢ **DNS** - Thanks to DNS nobody has to remember IP addresses – the **Domain Name System** is a hierarchical and decentralized naming system for computers, services, etc. connected to the internet or a private network. DNS works a bit like a telephone book: It assigns domain names like *www.univention.de* to numerical IP addresses (78.47.199.152) and vice versa. DNS consists of thousands of servers working together. If one server cannot resolve a name or IP, it can contact another server that can then ask the next one, and so on.

➢ **DHCP** (Dynamic Host Configuration Protocol) is a network protocol that is used to assign various network parameters to a device on the fly. This greatly simplifies administration of a network, since there is no need to assign static network parameters for each device. The DHCP server maintains a pool of available IP addresses and assign's one of them to the host.

➢ The **cloud** is a general metaphor that is used to refer to the delivery of different services and or resources through the Internet.

Figure 65 The metaphoric Cloud

These resources include tools and applications like data storage, servers, databases, networking, and software. Companies that provide cloud services enable users to store files and applications on remote servers and then access all the data via the Internet. This means the user is

 not required to be in a specific place (at their own computer) to gain access to it, allowing the user to work remotely. The actual **cloud** is a large capacity computer located in a backroom or a nondescript building somewhere.

Figure 66 A large capacity *Cloud* computer

A major component of the world wide web is Trans-Oceanic Cable Systems.

On 14 December **1988**, **TAT-8**, the first transatlantic optical fiber cable system was completed across the Atlantic. The 3,148 mile line was capable of handling **40,000** telephone calls simultaneously.

TAT-8 was built as a joint venture of AT&T, France Telecom, and British Telecom to connect the communications systems of France, Britain, and the United States. It could serve all three countries with a single line through the creation of an underwater branching unit. **TAT-8 was built at the cost of $335 million and operating from 1988 to 2002 and it** revolutionized communications.

Figure 67 Under Sea Fiber Optic Cable

The next transatlantic cable, **PTAT-1** was the first privately financed transatlantic fibre optic telecommunications cable, which was completed in **1989**, at a cost of **$400 million**. From this point, transoceanic cables were being installed quickly and their data transmission rates began to increase rapidly.

While the first fiber optic cable had a transmission rate of 280 megabits per second the next generation of optical fiber

amplifiers boosted data transmission rate of 5 Gigabits per second. Today's generation of undersea fiber optic systems are in the terabyte[43] range. About a 4000 to 1 increase.

Figure 68 Under Sea Optical Amplifier

---

[43] One Terabyte is 1024 gigabytes or 1,099,511,627,776 bytes

TeleGeography lists nearly 350 cables. Some of these cables cross oceans and others follow coasts down along continents. The whole network of submarine cables spans more than 550,000 miles, with some being buried as far underwater as Mount Everest towers above ground.

Over the last decade, however, global data consumption has exploded. In 2013, Internet traffic was 5 gigabytes per capita. This number is expected to reach 14 gigabytes per capita by 2018. New techniques in phase modulation and improvements in submarine line terminal equipment (SLTE) have boosted capacity in some places by as much as 8000 percent.

Figure 69 Cable Ship installing Fiber Optic Cable

f. The World Wide Web

This is what the
Internet
actually looks Like

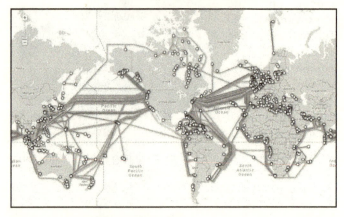

Figure 70 Undersea Fiber Optic systems have encircled the globe several times.

Currently 99% of the data traffic that is crossing oceans is carried by undersea cables. The reliability of submarine cables is high, especially when multiple paths are available in the event of a cable break. Also, the total carrying capacity of submarine cables is in the terabits per second, while satellites typically offer only 1,000 megabits per second and display higher latency[44]. However, a typical multi-terabit, transoceanic submarine cable system costs several hundred million dollars to construct.

---

[44] In computing, "latency" describes some type of delay. It typically refers to delays in transmitting or processing data,

The following is an illustration of what actually happens when a computer user in Chicago connects to a computer server[45] in London England:

The Chicago user sends and receives information on their computer screen. Their computer connects to a LAN, which communicates through a modem to the local Cable TV system offering internet access, such as AT&T, Cable Vision, etc..

From there, the back and forth information goes to a terrestrial communications network[46] which is connected to a number of web servers. From that web server, the information would go to the next web server, and the next server, and on and on, depending on the URL the information is destined to.

The information crosses the ocean over one of the undersea fiber optic cables. From there it goes through terrestrial cables and nodes in England until it gets to the destination's local Information Service Provider, in London. The information is then delivered to the modem and computer server (the computer where the actual web site is located).

It is amazing that the back and forth information generally, makes an incredibly long round trip in a blink of the eye.

Figure 71 The World wide Web is a collection of computer servers connected by high speed terrestrial cables

---

[45] A computer server is a computer which provides the functionality to multiple users, in other words the actual web site.
[46] This is the actual internet

Technically, the internet and the web are two different things, but the words are generally used interchangeably. The internet is the underlying support structure, which the Web uses to connect computer users to their desired websites. The Web provides the addresses, the URLs[47], of where the information is going and coming from and how to get there.

This is why all websites names, URLs, are registered in a common database.

---

[47] URL Uniform Resource Locator. A form of address that identifies the location on the World Wide Web of a page or file.

Chapter 5: Wireless

a. Radio

The **1930s** through the early **1950s** were called the **Golden Age of Radio.** Before television, radio provided entertainment by presenting radio plays and programs of mystery, soap operas, variety and comedy shows. There was also news and adventure series, like "The Lone Ranger" and "Superman".

In **1920**, the first commercially licensed radio station in the United States was KDKA in Pittsburgh began broadcasting. Virtually no one owned a radio set, but on election night that year, KDKA broadcast news of Warren G. Harding's victory in the presidential election, passing along returns phoned in from the local newspaper. The number of licensed broadcast stations rapidly surged from **5** in **1921** to **500** by **1924**. Radio quickly became a consumer craze. In **1930**, more than **40%** of American households owned a radio. A decade later that number more than doubled, to **83%**.

Figure 72 Family gathers to listen to weekly radio shows

The following excerpts from:
http://www.americanradioworks.org/segments/radio-the-internet-of-the-1930s/

> *The early public discussion of radios influence on society and culture reads much like the debates about the initial promises and dangers seen in the 21st century Internet revolution. Some predicted radio would be a powerful force for democratizing information and spreading knowledge to a vast population previously separated by*

geography or income. But the new technology also raised anxieties. Observers worried about the propriety and taste of the radio programs that would penetrate the sanctity of the home. Some critics of the radio fad worried that if families stayed home with the wireless it would erode civic involvement and compete with traditional social gatherings.

*Social scientists in the **1940s** and onward debated how significant radio's impact was in the decision-making process of the American voter. Some argued that radio was powerfully influential. Others contended that radio broadcasts on behalf of a candidate or party merely reinforced preconceived opinions. In the **1950s**, radio was eclipsed by television as a political forum. But in the years following FDRs presidency, no candidate for the White House could win without campaigning on the air.*

The following are excerpts from:
https://www.electronics-notes.com/articles/history/radio -receivers/radio-history-timeline.php

➢ **1901** *The First transatlantic transmission - on 12th December 1901 (with the successes in using radio waves to cross the English channel) Marconi turned his eyes towards being able to send messages across the Atlantic. If he could succeed in this he would be able to use his system to send messages across the Atlantic more cheaply than using a cable, and also keep in contact with ships over vast distances. Marconi had an antenna at Poldhu, England and a site in Newfoundland. The letter "S" being transmitted by the station in England was just received, although with great difficulty in Newfoundland .*

➢ **1930s Amplitude Modulation (AM)** *two-way mobile systems were in place in the U.S. that took advantage of newly developed mobile transmitters and utilized a "push-to-talk" or half-duplex transmission. By the end of the decade channel allocation grew from 11 to 40.*

➢ **1935** *The invention of **Frequency Modulation (FM)** improved audio quality. FM eliminated the need for* *large AM transmitters and resulted in radio equipment which required less power to operate. This made the use of transmitters in vehicles more practical.*

The following are excerpts from:
https://www.scienceabc.com/innovation/what-difference-fr equency-amplitude-modulation-radio-waves.html

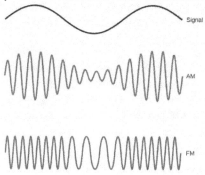

Figure 73 Audio signal shown with AM and FM modulation

Amplitude Modulation, *commonly abbreviated as **AM**, is a common method of broadcasting radio signals. This method dates back to the 1870s. In AM, the amplitude of the carrier wave is modified in order to transmit the input signal (the one that carries information).*
The amplitude of the carrier wave varies proportionally according to the input signal, so when the input signal has a low amplitude, the amplitude of the carrier wave is decreased and vice-versa.

Frequency Modulation, *often referred to as **FM** is another method of modulation where the carrier wave is modified proportionally, according to the input signal. In **FM**, the instantaneous frequency of the carrier wave is altered according to the amplitude of the input signal. Due to the much better transmission quality, most music radio stations prefer FM over AM to transmit information (mostly, songs) to their listeners.*

Back when people still used radios (instead of smart-phones and tablets) to tune in to the latest news and music on their

AM radios, the introduction of FM radio for commercial broadcasting was a really big deal. It was so important, in fact, that the term **FM** became synonymous with something that plays music; people still sometimes confuse the term **FM** with a device that plays music via radio waves.

➤ **1940s** The **Federal Communications Commission (FCC)** recognized a communication service it classified as Domestic Public Land Mobile (DPLM) radio service. The first DPLM system was established in St. Louis in **1946** and it utilized the 150 MHz band. The following year, a "highway" system was developed along the New York - Boston corridor using the 35-40 MHz band.

I. Amateur Radio

The following is from From Wikipedia, the free encyclopedia

➤ The origins of **Amateur Radio** can be traced to the late 19th century, but amateur radio as practiced today began in the early **20th century**. The First Annual Official Wireless Blue Book of the Wireless Association of America, produced in **1909**, contains a list of amateur radio stations. This radio callbook lists wireless telegraph stations in Canada and the United States, including 89 amateur radio stations. As with radio in general, amateur radio was associated with various amateur experimenters and hobbyists. **Amateur radio enthusiasts have significantly contributed to science, engineering, industry, and social services**. Research by amateur operators has founded new industries, built economies, empowered nations, and saved lives in times of emergency. Ham radio can also be used in the classroom to teach English, map skills, geography, math, science, and computer skills.

Figure 74 Amateur Radio Equipment

II. Walkie-Talkies

The following is from From Wikipedia, the free encyclopedia

*Canadian inventor Donald Hings was the first to create a portable radio signaling system for his employer CM&S in **1937**. This system later became known as a **walkie-talkie**. The Hings model C-58 **Handy-Talkie** was in military service by **1942**, which was the result of a secret R&D effort that began in **1940**. It was created by an engineering team in **1940** at the Galvin Manufacturing Company (the forerunner of Motorola).*

Figure 75 Military Portable Radio 1942

The Following are excerpts from:
https://www.vice.com/en_us/article/3daw98/the-story-of-f mx-a-wannabe-radio-standard-that-was-killed-in-a-very-pu blic-way

New York Times writer Jack Gould wrote around 1945

"Only the bounds of human imagination will place a limit on the usefulness of the 'walkie-talkie.' Its value will prove incalculable in reaching physicians while en route in automobiles to patients' homes, in providing contact for hunters with a central lodge, in directing delivery

trucks while they are in transit. All these services and many more are assuredly going to make life both more efficient, enjoyable and in many instances downright fun."

Figure 76 Modern Walkie-Talkies

III. Citizens band radio

The following is from From Wikipedia, the free encyclopedia

Citizens band radios (also known as CB radio) popularity spread into the general population in the US in the middle of the 1970s. CB Radios are used in many countries and is a short distance land mobile radio system. CB Radios, using two way radios operate on 40 channels near 27 MHz in the high frequency band. Citizens band is distinct from other personal radio service allocations such as FRS, GMRS, MURS, UHF CB and the Amateur Radio Service ("ham" radio). In many countries, CB operation does not require a license. Users on a channel must take turns talking. The transmitter's power is limited to 4 watts in the US and the EU, and CB radios have a range of about 3 to 20 miles, depending on terrain.

Figure 77 Citizens Band Radio - CB Radio

IV. Cordless Phone

In 1966, George Sweigert submitted a patent application for a "full duplex wireless communications apparatus". Also know as a cordless telephone or portable telephone is a telephone in which the handset is portable and communicates with the body of the phone by radio, instead of being attached by a cord. In 1994, digital cordless phones in the 900 MHz frequency range were introduced. Virtually all new telephones sold in the US use the 1.9 GHz, 2.4-GHz, or 5.8 GHz bands, though legacy phones can remain in use on the older bands. Some cordless phones advertised as 5.8 GHz actually transmit from base to phone on 5.8 GHz and transmit from phone to base on 2.4 GHz or 900 MHz, to conserve battery life.

Figure 78 Typical Cordless Phone

VI. WiFi

Wi-Fi is a wireless networking technology that allows computers and other devices to communicate over a wireless signal. WiFi is a "standard" defined by IEEE 802.11. There are differing opinions as to what the name **WiFi** stands for. To wit:

➤ **WiFi** is the name given IEEE 802.11 by the Wireless Ethernet Compatibility Alliance (WECA, now the **Wi-Fi Alliance**).

➤ The term also has been attributed to the IEEE 802.11 Working Group, with **Wi** referring to the fact that a wire traditionally served as the physical medium for LANs, and the homonym Fi referring to **PHY**, the PHYsical Layer of the OSI Reference Model. So, Wireless PHY became Wi-Fi.

➤ Although it must have been inspired by "high fidelity" (hi-fi), the name does not mean "wireless fidelity."

The following is from:
https://purple.ai/blogs/history-wifi/

> *WiFi was invented and first released for consumers in 1997, when a committee called IEEE802.11[48] was created. This set of standards defines communication for wireless local area networks (WLANs).*
>
> *In 2003, faster speeds and distance coverage of the earlier WiFi versions combined to make the 802.11g standard. Routers were getting better too, with higher power and further coverage than ever before. Home wireless routers are continuing to be improved.*

---

[48] The **Institute of Electrical and Electronics Engineers** is a professional association for electronic engineering and electrical engineering with its corporate office in New York City and its operations center in Piscataway, New Jersey. It was formed in 1963 from the amalgamation of the American Institute of Electrical Engineers and the Institute of Radio Engineers.

*The latest trend is called the **Internet of things (IOT)**, which means virtually everything in your home would communicate via the **WLAN**. Everything in the home, really means everything: the toaster, refrigerator, door bell, heating system, and on and on. According to Wi-FI.org, the Internet of Things (**IOT**) is "one of the most exciting waves of innovation the world has witnessed" and that **"its potential has only just begun to emerge."***

Figure 79 The Internet of things

b. Satellite

Today there are about 1,100 active satellites, both government and private. Also, there are about 2,600 satellites which are no longer work. The oldest one still in orbit, which is no longer functioning, was launched in **1958**.

The current batch of satellites has a wide variety of roles: GPS satellites aid in navigation, others relay telephone or television signals, others aid in weather forecasting, national defense, science, and agriculture, as in monitoring crops and areas of drought. The Union of Concerned Scientists, a private

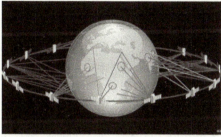

organization that maintains a database of satellites, says about 60 percent are used for communications.

Figure 80 Around 1100 active satellites currently around the earth

Communication satellites can be as big as a small school bus and weigh up to 6 tons. Most weigh a few tons or less. Some that are used briefly are 4 inch cubes and weigh about 2 pounds.

The location of the various satellites depends on their use. Communications satellites, which relay signals from a fixed spot on the equator, about 22,000 miles up. GPS satellites are at 12,400 miles, high enough to be accessible to large swaths of the Earth. Others that need a closer look at Earth are lower. For comparison, the International Space Station is only about 260 miles high, and very few satellites are lower than that. While some satellites remain over fixed spots on Earth, others fly over both poles or can move from place to place as needed.

All the satellites in orbit are owned by governments, large and small, and private companies. More than 50 countries own a satellite or a significant share in one.

There are agreed upon rules and recommendations for non-working satellites, which can pose a risk for collisions with active ones. Satellites that fly below a certain height are supposed to be put in an orbit that will make them fall to Earth and burn up within 25 years. At high altitudes, they are to be boosted up to still higher orbits to get them out of the way.

The following are excerpts from:
https://www.electronics-notes.com/articles/history/radio-r eceivers/radio-history-timeline.php

➢ *1945 Arthur C Clarke proposes geostationary satellites - Up until this time all international communications relied on either short wave radio transmissions or cable links. Short wave radio was unreliable and subject to high levels of interference, and international telephone cables were exceedingly expensive. In 1945 the author Arthur C Clarke wrote a historic article in Wireless World describing a system that used satellites in geostationary orbit. Signals would be transmitted up to the satellite that would rebroadcast them back to the earth. In view of their altitude above the earth the signals would be able to be received many thousands of miles away from the original transmitting station. Clarke calculated that only three satellites would be required to cover around the globe. His idea was revolutionary, and it took many years before the technology was available for it to be implemented.*

➢ *1957 Sputnik 1 launched - On 4th October 1957 the USSR (Russia) launched the first satellite into orbit. The satellite was in a very low orbit which took 96 minutes to circle the earth. It only transmitted a bleep, but it was sufficient to prove that satellites could be successfully put into orbit.*

➢ *1962 Telstar launched - Several other satellites followed Sputnik. Some were launched by the Soviet Union, and others by the Americans. However the launch of Telstar proved to be a major milestone in satellite development.*

➢ ***On 23rd July 1962,*** *Telstar was used to make the first live transatlantic television transmissions. Signals from the USA were seen live in many homes around Europe, making communications history. Another satellite named Relay was used to beam the pictures of the funeral of the Late President Kennedy to people all over the world. Since then the number of satellites has considerably increased, along with improvements in technology. Now most international communications are*  *routed via satellites. Apart from telecommunications, satellites provided many other useful functions including navigation, geological surveys, weather information, direct television broadcast and so forth.*

Figure 81 TelStar First US Communication Satellite

c. Television

Few inventions have had as much effect on contemporary American society as television.

The 1940s were the true beginning of the Television era. Although TV sets had been available as early as the late 1930s, the widespread distribution and sale of TV sets did not really take off until after World War II. Also, broadcasting stations neglected many of their radio stations and poured money into TV after the war.

Figure 82 Typical 1940s consumer TV

The following excerpts are from:
History of Television - Wikipedia, the free encyclopedia

> *Although all-electronic color TV was introduced in the U.S. in **1953**, high prices and the scarcity of color programming (TV shows) greatly slowed its acceptance in the marketplace. The first national color broadcast (the **1954** Tournament of Roses Parade) occurred on **January 1, 1954**, but during the following ten years, most network broadcasts, and nearly all local programming, continued to be in black-and-white. It was not until the **mid-1960s** that the color sets started selling in large numbers, due in part to the color transition of **1965** in which it was announced that over half of all network prime-time programming would be broadcast in color that fall. The first all-color prime-time season came just one year later. In **1972**, the last holdout among daytime network programs converted to color, resulting in the first complete all-color network season.*

*Digital television transition started in the late **2000s**. All the governments across the world set the deadline for analog shutdown by the **2010s**. Initially the adoption rate was low. But soon, more and more households were converted to digital televisions. The transition was completed worldwide by mid to late **2010s**.*

*A patent was filed in **1994** for an "intelligent" television system, linked with data processing systems, by means of a digital or analog network. Apart from being linked to data networks, one key point is its ability to automatically download necessary software routines, according to a user's demand, and process their needs.*

Smart TV *should not to be confused with Internet TV, IPTV or with Web TV.*

➢ ***Internet television*** *refers to the receiving television content over internet instead of traditional systems (terrestrial, cable and satellite) (although internet itself is received by these methods).*

➢ ***Internet Protocol television (IPTV)*** *is one of the emerging Internet television technology standards for use by television broadcasters.*

➢ ***Web television (WebTV)*** *is a term used for programs created by a wide variety of companies and individuals for broadcast on Internet TV.*

Cable television *is a system of broadcasting television programming to paying subscribers via radio frequency (RF) signals transmitted through coaxial cables or light pulses through fiber-optic cables. This contrasts with traditional terrestrial television, in which the television signal is transmitted over the air by radio waves and received by a television antenna attached to the television. FM radio programming, high-speed Internet, telephone service, and similar non-television services may also be provided through these cables. Early cable television was analog, but since the **2000s** all cable operators have switched to digital cable television.*

On **March 4, 1996** EchoStar introduced the Digital Sky Highway (Dish Network) using the EchoStar 1 satellite. EchoStar launched a second satellite in **September 1996** to increase the number of channels available on Dish Network to 170. These systems provided better pictures and stereo sound on 150-200 video and audio channels, and allowed small dishes to be used.

Service providers such as PrimeStar and DirecTV operate  at the higher frequency and power and therefore require much smaller dishes. However, one consequence of using the higher frequencies is **rain fade,** where viewers lose signal during a heavy downpour.

Figure 83 Typical Dish Antenna

Internet television (Internet TV), **(online television)** or IPTV **(Internet Protocol Television)** is the digital distribution of television content via the Internet as opposed to traditional systems like terrestrial, cable and satellite, although internet itself is received by terrestrial, cable or satellite methods. **Internet television** is a general term that covers the delivery of television shows and other video content over the Internet by video streaming technology, typically by major traditional television broadcasters.

By the late **2000s**, CRT[49] display technology was largely supplanted worldwide by flat-panel displays such as LCD[50]. Flat-panel television, especially LCD, has become the dominant form of television since the early **2010s**.

Before **1947** the number of U.S. homes with television sets could be measured in the thousands. By the late **1990s**, **98** percent of U.S. homes had at least one television set, and those sets were **on** for an average of more than seven hours a day.

---

[49] Cathode Ray Tube
[50] Liquid Crystal Display

The number of TV households in the United States in the TV season **2018/19** was estimated at **120 million**. While the number of TV households continues to grow, the number of pay TV households is on the decline. In **2015**, there were almost **100 million** pay TV households in the United States and this figure is projected to fall to **95 million** some time in **2020**.

d. Mobile Phone

Motorola in conjunction with the Bell System operated the first commercial mobile telephone service **Mobile Telephone Service (MTS)** in the US in **1946**, as a service of the Wire-Line Telephone Company.

Mobile radio-telephone systems were telephone systems of wireless type that preceded the modern cellular mobile form of telephony technology. These mobile telephones were usually mounted in cars or trucks (thus called car phones), although briefcase models were also made.

Some Mobile Phone Milestones:

➢ In **1947**, researchers began theorizing that a mobile telephone was possible. They experimented with installing telephones in vehicles. Scientists realized that by using small ranges of service areas while reusing frequency, they could be able to significantly increase the traffic capacity of mobile phones. It would take almost another 40 years before the world's first commercially-available mobile phone, the Motorola DynaTAC, was released.

➢ **1949** Radio Common Carriers (**RCCs**) were recognized.

➢ **1954** - Sony introduces the **first transistor radio** that sold for $49.95.

➢ **1957** - Soviet Union launches Sputnik, humanity's first artificial satellite

➢ **1964** AT&T introduces Improved Mobile Telephone System (**IMTS**).

➢ **1969** Nordic countries of Denmark, Finland, Iceland, Norway and Sweden agree to form a group to study and recommend areas of cooperation in telecommunication. This led to the standardization of telecommunications for all members of the **Nordic Mobile Telephone (NMT)**

group, the first comprehensive international standardization group.

➢ **1973** The NMT group specifies a feature allowing mobile telephones to be located within and across networks. This feature would become the basis for roaming.

➢ Advancements in Technology in the **1940s** and **1950s** led the development of cell towers that could receive signals from analog cell phones. This in turn led to the first car phones being installed in Limousines and other commercial vehicles. This new technology stunned the American public when it appeared in the **1954** Humphrey Bogart movie Sabrina.

Figure 84 Humphrey Bogart uses an Analog Cell Phone in 1954 movie.

e. Cell Phone

Some cell phone historical milestones:

➤ **On April 3, 1973, Motorola employee Martin Cooper stood in midtown Manhattan and placed a call (using the prototype) to the headquarters of Bell Labs in New Jersey. However, not until March 13, 1984,** somewhere in either Chicago, Baltimore or Washington, someone plunked down $3,995 to buy the Motorola DynaTAC 8000X, the first handheld. The phone weighed 1.75 pounds an had 30 minutes of talk time.

Figure 85 First Cell Phone call placed from Mid-Town Manhattan

➤ **1979** The FCC authorized the installation and testing of the first developmental cellular system in the US (Illinois Bell Telephone Company).

➤ **1981** Ericsson launches the world's first cellular system in Saudi Arabia based on the analog NMT 450 standard.

➤ **1991** The first digital cellular standard (GSM) is launched.

➤ By **1998** the number of mobile subscribers world-wide has grown to over 200 million.

The following are excerpts from:
https://www.brighthubengineering.com/diy-electronics-dev ices/3885-how-cell-phones-work/

> *Basically, the mobile phone is a radio. It relies on a radio signal in order to transmit and receive voice and data information. Previously, the radio device can only receive*

a signal from a commercial station, making it a one way communication apparatus. However, by integrating the principles behind Bell's telephone, the simple radio became a communication device which can also serve as a small transmitter thus giving it the capability to become a mobile phone.

Mobile phones are small radios embedded with mini transmitters. This means that it actually transmits radio signals when powered on.

This is a very important component because it readily gives up your electronic radio location so that calls can be diverted to you or make them.

One crucial part in the mobile phone communication is the establishment of relay centers called "base stations". These stations are actually smaller versions of transmitter towers that you will see around the neighborhood in almost any places. The base station serves as the electronic bridge between two mobile phones.

The principle is basically simple, because your mobile phone transmits a certain amount of radio signal, whatever base station nearest to you will capture its presence. Therefore, this gives you an "always online" mode ready to receive calls and texts. When another mobile phone user wants to contact you, their mobile phone will transmit a signal to the nearest base station in their location. This base station will then transmit to a series of telecommunication relay equipment such as channel towers or satellites until it reaches your local base station wherever you are. The same procedure goes when you are the one to call out to another number.

When the user dials a particular number, the base station will automatically identify that number and assign an encrypted code on its transmission. Therefore, when the stations send out transmissions, it will only be transmitted to the shortest possible relays that will connect to the exact number you have dialed.

The term cell phone is derived from the "cell" principle of radio transmission. Each base station provides a single **"cell"** or **radio signal span radius**. Combining all of these signals in a location makes it appear as cellular compartments. Therefore, when you change your location, you go out of a single cell and enter a new one. With each change in the phone's location, the base station nearest to you will provide you a signal. In some cases, you may arrive at a location when no signal from any base stations is present; this is called a "dead spot".

The following furthers explanation of how and why **cells** allow thousands of phones to work at the same time.

The following excerpts are taken from:
https://www.explainthatstuff.com/cellphones.html

A cell phone automatically communicates with the nearest cell (the one with the strongest signal) and uses as little power to do so as it possibly can (which makes its battery last as long as possible and reduces the likelihood of it interfering with other phones nearby).

If the phones all send and receive calls in the same way, using the same kind of radio waves, the signals would interfere and scramble together and it would be impossible to tell one call from another. If each phone call uses a slightly different **frequency**, the calls are easy to keep separate.

That's fine if there are only a few people are calling at once. But suppose you're in the middle of a big city and millions of people are all calling at once. Then you'd need just as many millions of separate frequencies, more than are usually available. The solution is to divide the city up into smaller areas, with each one served by its own antenna and base station. These areas are what we call **cells** and they look like a patchwork of invisible hexagons. Each cell has its base station and antenna and all the calls made or received inside that cell are routed through them. Cells enable the system to handle many more calls at once, because each cell uses the same set of frequencies as its neighboring cells. The more cells, the *greater the number of calls that can be made at once. This is why urban areas have many more cells than rural areas and why the cells in urban areas are much smaller.*

*If a phone in cell **A** calls a phone in cell **B**, the call doesn't pass directly between the phones, but from the first phone to antenna **A** and its base station, then to antenna **B** and its base station, and then to the second phone.*

Cellphones that are moving between cells (when people are walking along or driving) are regularly sending signals to and from nearby antennas so that, at any given time, the cell phone network always knows which antenna is closest to which phone.

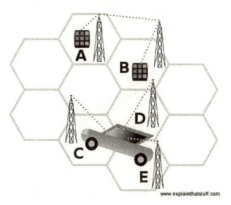

www.explainthatstuff.com

Figure 86 Cell Phone Network of Cell Towers

If a car passenger is making a call and the car drives between cells C, D, and E, the phone call is automatically "handed off" (passed from cell to cell) so the call is not interrupted.

I. Advances in Cellular network systems:

➢ In the 1990's the 2nd generation mobile phones emerged. The second generation introduced text messaging. 2G also introduced the ability to access media on mobile phones.

➢ The main difference between 3G technology from 2G technology is the use of packet switching rather than circuit switching for data transmission. The first 3G network was launched in Japan. By the end of 2007 there were 295 million subscribers on the 3G network.

➢ The main ways in which 4G differed, technologically from 3G was in its elimination of circuit switching, instead employing an all-IP network. 4G is faster then the previous networks.

➢ After the success of 4G LTE, new requirements started to surface for many applications from high speed, very low latency to very low speed data. 5G was developed around *use cases* rather than a requirement for faster speed and its introduction is expected by 2020 with some early reduced sets were introduced in late 2018.

Chapter 6: Other notable advances

While the cellular networks were improving, advances in the cell phone itself were occurring. More and more functionality was being added to the cell phone as well, from the 1980's thru to today. Various areas of electronic component advances had been occurring in parallel during this time period. **Note** that these individual technologies were not being developed for the cell phone, most started out as stand alone products. But were eventually adapted to the cell phone. Some examples of these stand alone products are:

a. Touch Screen:

➢ **Touch Screen** - Historians consider the first touch screen to be a capacitive touch screen invented by E.A. Johnson at the Royal Radar Establishment, Malvern, UK, around **1965 - 1967**.

➢ In the year of **1983** a new touchscreen was developed by Bell Labs. These were called the Soft machines, and they were seen as a reliable and faster system for touch screen computers.

Figure 87 Bell Labs Touch Screen

> Also in **1983,** Apple designed a prototype for a landline telephone set with a built-in touchscreen. The device featured a touchscreen but it had a monochrome look and implemented a stylus for input.

Figure 88 Apple Touch Screen land line Phone

> The IBM Simon was the first phone with a touchscreen in **1992.**, which featured a calendar, notepad, and fax function, and a touch screen interface that allowed users to dial phone numbers.

Figure 89 IBM's Simon Personal Communicator Phone

> In **1993**, Apple released the Newton PDA[51], equipped with handwriting recognition

> In **1996**, Palm entered the PDA market and advanced touch screen technology with its Pilot series.

---

[51] Personal Digital Assistant

> The first graphic tablet resembling contemporary tablets and used for handwriting recognition by a computer was the *Stylator* in **1957**. Digitizers were popular in the mid-**1970s** and early **1980s** by the commercial success of the ID (Intelligent Digitizer) and BitPad manufactured by the Summagraphics Corp.

> In **1983** the first home computer graphic tablet was the  Kola Pad. Though originally designed for the Apple II, the Kola eventually broadened its applicability to practically all home computers with graphic support, examples of which include the TRS-80 Color Computer, Commodore 64, and Atari 8-bit family.

Figure 90 Kola Pad - Graphics Tablet

> In 2007, Apple released the most innovated touchscreen technology anyone had yet seen. The iPhone interface is completely touch-based, including the notorious virtual keyboard. Apple's line of I-Phones led to other devices like the iPod Touch and the iPad.

> Launched in 2010 This graphics tablet from Monoprice is one of the best selling budget graphics tablets on the market

Figure 91 Monoprice MP1060-HA60 Graphic Drawing Table

b. Pin Camera:

➢ The CCD[52] camera was invented in **1969** at Bell Labs by Willard Boyle and George Smith. **The CCD became the bedrock of the digital image revolution,** including digital photography and video.

Figure 92 CCD Camera developed at Bell Labs

➢ The first commercial CCD camera was developed by Fairchild in **1976**. The following year Konica introduced the C35-AF, the world's first compact point-and-shoot autofocus camera. But the film-less age was kick started in **1981**, when Sony demonstrated the first camera to bear the name Mavica (Magnetic Video Camera).

➢ The Apple QuickTake 100, launched in **1994**, was actually manufactured by Kodak, and was the first

colour digital camera for under $1,000. It packed a 640x480-pixel CCD and could store up to eight images in the internal memory.

Figure 93 Apple Quick-Take camera

---

[52] Fundamentally, a charge coupled device (CCD) is an integrated circuit forming light sensitive elements called pixels. Photons hitting this surface generate a charge that can be read by electronics and turned into a digital copy of the light patterns falling on the device. In other words a picture.

➢ The Canon PowerShot 600 released in **1996**, had a 1/3-inch, 832x608-pixel CCD, built-in flash, auto white balance and an optical viewfinder as well as an LCD display. It was the first consumer digital camera able to write images to a hard disk drive, and could store up to 176MB. It cost $949.

➢ The first cell phone with a built-in camera was manufactured by Samsung and released in South Korea in **2000**. The SCH-V200 flipped open to reveal a 1.5-inch TFT-LCD, and the built-in digital camera was capable of  taking 20 photos at 350,000-pixel resolution, which is 0.35-megapixels, but it had to hook up to a computer to get the photos. The camera and the phone components were essentially separate devices housed in the same body.

Figure 94 Samsung SGH-V200 Cell Phone w/Camera

➢ In **2002** the Sanyo SCP-5300 was introduced in the US. It cost $400 and it featured a clamshell design. With a 0.3-megapixel capability, it could capture shots at 640 x 480 pixels. By the end of **2003**, camera phones were really taking off in the U.S. and over 80 million had already been sold worldwide.

c. Vibration, tilt and acceleration

A wide range of sensors and transducers are based on what is called a piezoelectric crystal effect. The word *piezoelectricity* means electricity resulting from pressure and latent heat. It is derived from the Greek word *piezein*, which means to squeeze or press, and *ēlektron*, which means amber, an ancient source of electric charge.

The piezoelectric effect was discovered by Jacques and Pierre Curie in **1880**. They found that pressure applied to a quartz crystal creates an electric charge in the crystal, a phenomenon they referred to as the (direct) piezoelectric effect.

The exact opposite was also discovered, that connecting the crystal to an electrical source would cause the crystal to deform.

As it turned out, the applications of the piezoelectric devices are seemingly endless.

Figure 95 Circa 1880 Piezoelectric in a test fixture

An **accelerometer** is a device that measures the vibration, or

acceleration of motion of a structure. The force caused by vibration or a change in motion (acceleration) causes the mass to "squeeze" the piezoelectric material which produces an electrical charge that is proportional to the force exerted upon it.

Figure 96 Three axis accelerometer

Piezoelectric Printers - Generally speaking, there are two main types of printers that use piezoelectric actuators:

A **dot-matrix printer** uses piezoelectric actuators in the printer head move needle-like pins that "poke" through a strip of ink tape (similar to a typewriter) against a piece of paper in various patterns to form characters.

An **ink-jet printer** uses piezoelectric actuators in the printer head act on small diaphragms or otherwise change the geometry of an inkwell so that ink droplets are forced out of an orifice onto paper. This is one of the dominant technologies in the printer market to date.

Piezoelectric Speakers - Piezoelectric speakers are featured in virtually every application that needs to efficiently produce sound from a small electronic gadget. These types of speakers are usually inexpensive and require little power to produce relatively large sound volumes. Thus, piezoelectric speakers are often found in devices such as:

Cell phones
Ear buds
Sound-producing toys
Musical greeting cards

Piezoelectric Buzzers - Piezoelectric buzzers are similar to piezoelectric speakers, but they are usually designed with lower fidelity to produce a louder volume over a narrower frequency range. Buzzers are used in a seemingly endless array of electronic devices, such as:

Intruder Alarms
Medical Devices
PIN Pads
Alarm clocks
Wristwatch Alarms
Fire Alarms
Microwave Ovens
Ultra Sonic Insect Repellers

Accelerometers are used to measure the motion and vibration from a variety of sources, including:

Human activities - walking, running or exercising
Construction work - driving piles, demolition, drilling and excavating
Vehicle collisions

Impact loads - falling debris
Concussion loads - internal and external explosions
Collapse of structural elements
Wind loads and wind gusts measurements
Earthquakes and aftershocks measurement

The **Segway PT** is a two-wheeled, self-balancing personal transporter manufactured by Segway Inc. It was invented by Dean Kamen and brought to market in **2001**.

The **Self-Balancing Electric Scooter** uses a built-in gyroscope and a sensor (accelerometer) pad. By tilting the pad the rider can control the speed and direction of travel. Shane Chen, an American businessman filed a patent for a device of this type in February **2013**.

Figure 97 Self-Balancing Scooter

The Pedometer

Figure 98 Typical Pedometer

The following are excerpts from :
https://en.wikipedia.org/wiki/Pedometer

> *A mechanical **pedometer** obtained from France was introduced in the US by Thomas Jefferson. It is not known if he modified the design; although this pedometer is widely attributed to Jefferson*

> *In **1965** a pedometer called a manpo-kei (meaning "10,000 steps meter" was marketed in Japan by Y. Hatano. Y. Hatano promoted "manpo-kei pedometers" from **1985**, after his research was accepted.*

*The technology for a pedometer includes a mechanical sensor and software to count steps. Early forms used a mechanical switch to detect steps together with a simple counter. If one shakes these devices, one hears a lead ball sliding back and forth, or a pendulum striking stops as it swings. Today advanced step counters rely on MEMS inertial sensors and sophisticated software to detect steps. These **MEMS**[53] sensors have either 1-, 2- or 3-axis detection of acceleration.*

Some **Piezoelectric** patents:

The following are excerpts from:
https://www.explainthatstuff.com/piezoelectricity.html

Inventors have been dreaming up all kinds of imaginative uses for piezoelectricity for years. Here are a few examples from the US Patent and Trademark Office database:

- *US Patent: US 20140128753 A1: Piezoelectric heart rate sensing for wearable devices or mobile devices by Michael Edward Smith Luna et al, 8 May **2014**. A cutting-edge sensor that can monitor your heart and send details to your cell phone (or similar mobile device).*

- *US Patent: 8,087,186: Piezoelectric-based toe-heaters for frostbite protection by ⌐ Jahangir S. Rastegar, 3 January **2012**. These shoes use piezoelectric materials to convert the repeated squashing and stretching of your shoes into electrical energy that can warm your feet.*

- *US Patent: 20050127677: Roadway generating electrical power by incorporating piezoelectric materials by Jeffrey Luttrull, 16 June **2005**. Describes a method of harvesting energy from roads. US Patent: 8,278,800: Multi-layer piezoelectric generator by Haim Abramovich et al, Innowattech, 2 October **2010**, is a*

---

[53] **Microelectromechanical systems** are the technology of microscopic devices, particularly those with moving parts. It merges at the nanoscale into nanoelectromechanical systems (NEMS) and nanotechnology.

variation on the same basic idea with more details of how road generators would actually work.

- *US Patent: 4,685,296: Ocean wave energy conversion using piezoelectric material members by Joseph R. Burns, 11 August **1987**. In this invention, piezoelectric materials generate electricity from the up-and-down movements of ocean waves.*

- *US Patent: 5,598,196: Piezoelectric ink jet print head and method of making by Hilarion Braun, Eastman Kodak, 28 January **1987**. An inkjet print head that squirts precise droplets of ink using piezoelectric materials.*

Introduced in **2009** the first smart phone to make use of an accelerometer was Apple's iPhone 3GS with the introduction of such features as the compass app and shake to undo, according to Wired magazine.

Chapter 7: Global Positioning

On June 26, 1993, the U.S. Air Force launched the 24th Navstar satellite into orbit, completing a network of 24 satellites known as the Global Positioning System, or GPS. With a GPS receiver that costs less than a few hundred dollars you can instantly learn your location on the planet your latitude, longitude, and even your altitude to within a few hundred feet.

The **Global Positioning System (GPS)**, originally **NAVSTAR GPS**, is a satellite-based radionavigation system owned by the United States government and operated by the United States Air Force. It is a global navigation satellite system (GNSS) that provides geolocation[54] and time information to a GPS receiver anywhere on or near the Earth where there is an unobstructed line of sight to four or more GPS satellites. Obstacles such as mountains and buildings block the relatively weak GPS signals.

In total, there are 31 operational satellites in the GPS constellation, with 3-5 additional satellites in reserve that can be activated when needed. The satellites circle the Earth two times a day at 20,200 km (12,550 miles) up. The U.S. Air Force monitors and manages the system, and has committed to having at least 24 satellites available for 95% of the time.

A **GPS** device allows you to easily and safely navigate your drive around town or cross country. You can also add ease to your outdoor activities with a golf **GPS** or handheld device for outdoor adventures.

The **GPS project** was started by the U.S. Department of Defense in **1973**, with the first prototype spacecraft launched

---

[54] Geolocation is the process of finding, determining and providing the exact location of a computer, networking device or equipment. It enables device location based on geographical coordinates and measurements

in **1978** and the full constellation of **24** satellites operational in **1993** and cost taxpayers $12 billion. Originally limited to use by the United States military, civilian use was allowed from the **1980s**.

The **GPS** project was launched to overcome the limitations of previous navigation systems, integrating ideas from several predecessors, including classified engineering design studies from the **1960s**.

The design of GPS is based partly on a similar ground-based radio-navigation systems, such as **LORAN**[55] and the **Decca Navigator**[56], developed in the early **1940s**.

Figure 99 Diagram of GPS "constellation"

---

[55] LORAN, short for long range navigation, was a radio navigation system developed in the United States during World War II.
[56] The Decca Navigator System was a radio navigation system which allowed ships and aircraft to determine their position by receiving radio signals from fixed navigational beacons.

The GPS technology was made possible by a combination of scientific and engineering advances, particularly the development of the world's most accurate timepieces: atomic clocks[57] that are precise to within a billionth of a second. The clocks were created by physicists seeking answers to questions about the nature of the universe, with no conception that their technology would some day lead to a global system of navigation. Today, GPS is saving lives, helping society in countless other ways, and generating 100,000 jobs in a multi-billion-dollar industry.

In **1989**, the first consumer GPS was developed by Magellan. The NAV 1000 was 1.5 pounds, cost $3,000 and could run for a couple hours at a time on battery power. As GPS accuracy improved, many different industries could take advantage of GPS technology. GPS tracking is much more affordable these days. GPS trackers are lightweight and can fit in the palm of your hand.

For many, using a GPS device in the car to navigate traffic or having GPS location in their smart-phone is now just part of daily life. We are so comfortable with this technology that we take it for granted.

---

[57] Atomic clocks are the most accurate time and frequency standards known, and are used as primary standards for international time distribution services, to control the wave frequency of television broadcasts, and in global navigation satellite systems such as GPS.

a. How does the GPS work ?

The following are excerpts from:
http://www.physics.org/article-questions.asp?id=55

Wherever you are on the planet, at least four GPS satellites are visible to you at any time. Each satellite transmits information about its position and the current time at regular intervals. These signals, are received by your GPS device, which calculates how far away each satellite is, based on how long it took for the messages to arrive.

Imagine you are standing somewhere on Earth with three satellites in the sky above you. If you know how far

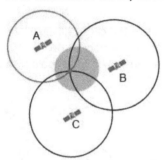

away you are from satellite A, then you know you must be located somewhere in circle A. If you do the same for satellites B and C, you can work out your location by seeing where the three circles intersect.

Figure 100 Three GPS location calculations

This is just what your GPS receiver does, although it uses overlapping spheres rather than circles.

Once it has information on how far away, at least three satellites are, your GPS receiver can pinpoint your location using a process called trilateration[58]

---

[58] The measurement of the lengths of the three sides of a series of touching or overlapping triangles on the earth's surface for the determination of the relative position of points by geometrical means (as in geodesy, map making, and surveying)

The more satellites there are above the horizon the more accurately your GPS unit can determine where you are.

1995: Navsys was contracted to integrate GPS positioning into a cell phone so that location information could be sent to a communications center for mobile 911 calls. Developed by Navsys Corporation, is now on display at the Smithsonian National Air and Space Museum's Time and Navigtion exhibition. This device marks an important step in GPS history that paved the way for positioning to become the integral component of communications technology that exists today.

1999: The first commercially available phone with GPS was the Benefon, released In Europe.

2004: Qualcomm introduced assisted GPS technology, allowing phones to use the cellular signal in combination with GPS signal to locate the user to within a few feet. This is the primary model for the current generation of smart phone GPS

Aside from giving drivers turn by turn directions to a particular address location and help avoid traffic backups, the GPS is solving crimes and provide security.

The following are excerpts from:
https://www.trackerreviews.net/gps-trackers-are-preventing-crime/

> *Over the years, advanced GPS technology has been able to help people keep a better eye on their valuable property by giving them real time location reports on the current location of their tracker. Not only can you track vehicles, you can also track valuable assets, equipment, shipments etc. With the historical route playback feature that most GPS companies offer, this gives the user the ability to present a summary of all the places the tracker has been, enhancing the credibility of the source.*

The following are excerpts from:
https://www.trackerreviews.net/personal-gps-tracking-for-travelers/

> *There are plenty of companies that provide GPS trackers small enough to be worn in a pocket or bag. With the*

power of GPS satellites, the tracking devices can track a person down to which street they are on, where they have been, and even how long they stopped for. Whether it is for a parent whose child is traveling away from home for the first time, or a friend making sure you get to your new job in Europe safely, GPS trackers can give you an extra level of security.

Chapter 8: The rise of the machines

Many of the technological developments over the past 70 years or so, became a significant and game changing advancement on their own. Perhaps, initially by happenstance, a version of many of these technologies ended up being put into the smart cell phone. In other word without the advancements that came before it the cell phone would not be quite what it is today, Some of the milestone in the cell phone evolution are listed below:

➤ **1983:** the world got the first ever portable mobile phone in the shape of the Motorola DynaTAC 8000X. It cost $4000 USD and was a huge status symbol at the time. In 1989 Motorola followed up the DynaTAC with the 9800X or MicroTAC, it came with a fold down keyboard cover and set the standard for the flip phone form factor seen throughout the 90's.

➤ **1992:** Mobiles were no longer restricted to business use. Mass production paved the way for cost-effective consumer handsets with digital displays. Nokia was one of the first to take advantage of this transition, with the Nokia 1011 arriving that year.

➤ **1996:** The mobile phone industry was revolutionized by Motorola when it launched the world's first flip phone, otherwise known as a "clamshell" phone, on January 3, 1996. The Motorola StarTAC was an instant success, garnering widespread popularity among mobile users. During its release, the StarTAC became the smallest, lightest handset in the market at 3.1 ounces. Some of the key features of the StarTAC included SMS text messages, vibrate alert setting and the use of lithium-ion battery as back-up battery.

➤ **1995 - 1998:**   Although it only offered four colors, the Siemens S10 brought mobile phone displays to life for the first time in 1997. The same year Hagenuk launched the GlobalHandy, the first device without an external aerial. The following year Nokia launched a range of Xpress-on interchangeable covers of the 5100 series, making it the first fashion orientated phone.

➢ **1999:** The BlackBerry was introduced. It offered something all its competitors couldn't touch - access to emails on the go. Even if you didn't own a Blackberry, you knew someone that did, or that you would at least see one in the hands of someone else on a regular basis. Those days are gone and while BlackBerry may still have millions of users, it's lost its mojo.

➢ **1999:** Nokia unveiled the 7110 which was the first device to take advantage of WAP (a means of accessing information over a mobile wireless network). A year later Sharp launched the world's very first camera phone, the J-SH04. It was only available in Japan, but it signaled the start of the public's obsession with phone photography. However, it was not until **2002** and the release of the Sony Ericsson T68i and its clip-on camera, that western markets started to take an interest in the camera phone.

➢ **2003 - 2006:** The implementation of 3G took download speeds up to 2MBS. RIM brought mobile email to the masses with its range of the popular BlackBerry devices like the 8100 Pearl. The advent of front facing cameras in 2003 on devices such as the Sony Ericsson Z1010 meant video calling became possible, but not popular.

➢ **2007 - 2010:** Swiping and scrolling replaced the traditional button method of input. The LG Prada is the first touchscreen to market ahead of the Apple iPhone in May 2007. However, Apple proved to have both the stronger brand and superior knowledge of capacitive touchscreen's potential.

➢ **2011 - 2014:** Smart-phones became increasingly central to modern life, offering much more than just communication features. The first 4G service in the UK launched in 11 cities by in 2012 increasing download speeds up to 12mbps. Voice recognition became common place, first with Google Voice before Apple launched Siri into the market. Samsung added a built-in heart rate monitor to their flagship Galaxy S5 to capitalize on the growth in mobile health & fitness.

- ➤ **2015 - 2018:** The global adoption of 4G vastly improves video streaming and video calling capabilities. Screen sizes continue to grow to maximize the experience of these features, with the iPhone 7 Plus display now 57% larger than the original iPhone from 2007. Mobile payments also emerge with Apple Pay and Android Pay offering users the possibility of buying things with their smart-phone.

- ➤ **Present Day:** The fifth-generation network promises vastly superior data speeds and reliability, boosting ultra-high-resolution video streaming and mobile gaming. Handset design trends continue to push for an all-screen experience, with OnePlus introducing the pop-up selfie camera to its flagship 7 Pro device.

Much more historical information about cell phones can be found of the web. For an example: **The Evolution of mobile phones: 1973 to 2019 by Daniel Dudley Nov. 2018** *https://flauntdigital.com/blog/evolution-mobile-phones/*

a. The rise of the APPs

As with most high tech advances, the more the device can do for you, the more popular it becomes. The *Applications* for smart phones has exploded and therefore the use of cell phones. A mobile app is a software application. Basically, it is a computer generated program designed and developed to run on iPhone, Smart-phones, tablets and many other mobile devices. Most people have smart phones and I-Phones today, so apps are easy to access and simply make your life better as a result. There are millions of mobile apps at present. For examples, apps for social networks, travel, health, banking, fitness, calendars, games, news and much more. The Apple App store adds more than 20,000 apps every month.

The app market is seeing the revenue of more than $30 billion yearly and still growing. The year of 2014 was witnessed over 138 million app downloads in a single year, with an estimation of downloads reaching 268 million in 2017.

According to a research firm: Flurry Analytic:

- ➢ Total iPhone app downloads: **30 billion**
- ➢ Total Android app downloads: **15 billion**
- ➢ An average number of apps per smart-phone user: **41**

Today, the machines (smart phones) have become an integral and generally an important part of our lives. Many people use them for work, shopping, banking, watching sports or seeing who just rang the door bell at home. The *machines* are obviously very useful in our daily lives and can literally save lives.

In social media, the smart phone is the preferred communication method between teenagers (even when they are standing next to each other). In fact, we are so attached to our smart phone that some, old and young alike, may suffer withdrawals if their smart phones are taken away. Some using their cell phones, walk into walls, railings and other people while ignoring the "real" world around them.

People have always been enamoured with technology, from the rotary dial telephone and home radios in the 1940s, watching TV in the 1950s, personal computers in the 1980s and smart phones in 2000s. It does seem as though the enthusiasm for the smart phone is even greater than previous technologies. But rest assured we will be enamoured in the future with the next technological advance.

By the way, one popular use of the smart phone is to take pictures of our food and share the picture with all of our friends. So while the technology changes people haven't really changed.

Case in point, the ancient Egyptians put pictures of their meals on walls, along with the recipes.

Table of Figures

References

https://www.history.com/news/11-innovations-that-c hanged-history

How it works.com/transistors

CED in the History of Media Technology

www.historyofinformation.com

https://www.computerhistory.org

https://www.theclever.com/15-huge-supercomputers-tha t-were-less-powerful-than-your-smartphone/

Wikipedia, the free encyclopedia: An integrated circuit or monolithic integrated circuit

ethw.org/Milestones:First_Semiconductor_Integrated_Circu i t_(IC),_1958

https://www.computerhistory.org/timeline/1942/

https://www.computerhope.com/jargon/m/mainfram.htm

Wikipedia ,the free encyclopedia: A punched card

https://www.computerhope.com/jargon/p/punccard.h tm

Wikipedia, the free encyclopedia : A minicomputer

http://www.science.smith.edu/~jcardell/Courses/EGR328/R eadings/uProc%20Ovw.pdfA

https://medium.com/swlh/the-past-present-and-future-of-s peech-recognition-technology-cf13c179aaf

http://www.ancientpages.com/2016/03/04/fascinating-anc ient-history-of-fingerprints/

Wikipedia, the free encyclopedia - Computer mouse

Techwalla
*https://www.techwalla.com/articles/the-history-of-comput
er-scanners*

Wikipedia, the free encyclopedia - Computer Scanners

Wikipedia, the free encyclopedia - Optical Character Recognition

thoughtco.com/history-of-computer-memory-1992372.
https://www.thoughtco.com/history-of-computer-memor
y-1992372

https://computer.howstuffworks.com/computer-memory2.
htm

https://www.computerhistory.org/siliconengine/semicondu
ctor-read-only-memory-chips-appear/

Wikipedia ,the free encyclopedia : The History of Hard Disk
Drives

Wikipedia, the free encyclopedia : Removable media

Wikipedia, the free encyclopedia : File Allocation Table

https://www.computerhope.com/history/printer.htm

https://www.realtor.com/news/trends/3-d-printed-homes/

https://lowendmac.com/2014/personal-computer-history-t
he-first-25-years/

https://en.wikipedia.org/wiki/History_of_software

Wikipedia, the free encyclopedia : Assembly Language

Wikipedia, the free encyclopedia : BASIC (Beginner's
All-purpose Symbolic Instruction Code)

Wikipedia, the free encyclopedia : History of UNIX

Wikipedia ,the free encyclopedia : MS-DOS (Microsoft Disk
Operating System)

Top 10 Most Important Software Programs by John C.
Dvorak 2004

https://bebusinessed.com/history/history-of-the-telephone

http://www.telephonetribute.com/timeline.html

http://www.americanradioworks.org/segments/radio-the-internet-of-the-1930s/

https://www.electronics-notes.com/articles/history/radio-receivers/radio-history-timeline.php

https://www.scienceabc.com/innovation/what-difference-fr equency-amplitude-modulation-radio-waves.html

Wikipedia,the free encyclopedia : The origins of Amateur Radio

Wikipedia, the free encyclopedia : Walkie-Talkies

https://www.vice.com/en_us/article/3daw98/the-story-of-fmx-a-wannabe-radio-standard-that-was-killed-in-a-very-public-way

Wikipedia,the free encyclopedia : Citizens band radios

https://purple.ai/blogs/history-wifi/

https://www.electronics-notes.com/articles/history/radio-receivers/radio-history-timeline.php

Wikipedia, the free encyclopedia : History of Television

https://www.brighthubengineering.com/diy-electronics-devices/3885-how-cell-phones-work/

https://www.explainthatstuff.com/cellphones.html

https://en.wikipedia.org/wiki/Pedometer

https://www.explainthatstuff.com/piezoelectricity.html

http://www.physics.org/article-questions.asp?id=55

https://www.trackerreviews.net/gps-trackers-are-preventing-crime/

https://www.trackerreviews.net/personal-gps-tracking-fort ravelers/

www.ingramcontent.com/pod-product-compliance
Lightning Source LLC
Chambersburg PA
CBHW031221050326
40689CB00009B/1423